PRIMARY
FOUNDATIONS

History

AGES 5-7

Keith Andreetti
and Karin Doull

CONTENTS

Authors
Keith Andreetti and
Karin Doull

Editor
Clare Gallaher

Assistant Editor
Roanne Davis

Series Designer
Lynne Joesbury

Designer
Paul Roberts

Illustrations
Geoff Jones

Cover photograph
Getty One Stone

Published by Scholastic Ltd,
Villiers House,
Clarendon Avenue,
Leamington Spa,
Warwickshire
CV32 5PR
Visit our website at www.scholastic.co.uk
Text © 2000 Keith Andreetti and Karin Doull © 2000 Scholastic Ltd

1 2 3 4 5 6 7 8 9 0
0 1 2 3 4 5 6 7 8 9

British Library Cataloguing-in-Publication Data
A catalogue record for this book is available from the British Library.

ISBN 0-439-01789-0

The right of Keith Andreetti and Karin Doull to be identified as the Authors of this work has been asserted by them in accordance with the Copyright, Designs and Patents Act 1988.

Introduction

This book suggests how history can be divided into manageable teaching units for five- to seven-year-olds. Each themed chapter provides two units of work (with the exception of Chapter 5, which has just one). These units are often complementary to each other and therefore you should choose one or other as appropriate to your needs. Most of the units can be used to form the basis of a substantial chunk of history work – perhaps over a half term – and by providing progressive lesson plans show how history can be sequenced. The grids at the beginning of each unit are intended to aid medium-term planning. They highlight (in bold) the enquiry questions covered by the lesson plans as well as additional enquiry questions which could be used to extend the unit further. The grids can also be used to help plan links that history has with other subjects across the curriculum, especially literacy and numeracy. (ICT links are given within the lesson plans themselves.) By providing a broad overview, the grids also help with planning the resources that you will need to collect in preparation for the unit.

The introduction to each chapter provides some background information that you may find useful when working with the lesson plans, and further information is given in the lesson plans themselves, where necessary.

Why is history important?

Before a subject can be taught well the teacher must understand what is most important and why it is important. History sometimes suffers from the fact that teachers do not always stop to consider its purpose. It is just 'there'. The National Curriculum Handbook for teachers starts the history section with four quotations that give some very good reasons for teaching history. They can be summarised as follows:

● History is about people; it allows us to examine the ways people behave, the ways in which they live and the things that happen to them and shows us that we belong to a rich tapestry of humanity.

● History is the science of story; it requires us to analyse and evaluate, to examine points of view and deduce motivation, to argue about morality and pronounce on character, all in the exciting virtual world of the past.

● History is about identity; it shows us why the world is as it is and presents our common heritage from which we can choose the elements on which to model ourselves and the world we want to create.

● History has endless content, and it can provide high-quality material for developing literacy, artistic and musical skills and can often link strongly with other subjects in the curriculum.

History for five- to seven-year-olds

The Key Stage 1 teacher has two main priorities in teaching history. The first is to lay the foundations of historical skills and understanding, and monitor progression in them. The second is to lay down some markers of stories and factual information that will help children to navigate the great oceans of the past. The lesson plans given in this book have learning objectives which are designed to develop the required abilities in children, and the content of the activities is based on solid historical evidence.

Skills and understanding
1 Chronological understanding

The primary tool for placing events and objects in chronological order is the timeline. A simple timeline will have only two stages: old object – new object, or, a picture of child as a baby – a picture of the child now. Timelines may be representative of short or long periods of time; children can sequence their own day (*I get out of bed, I come to school, I do my work* and so on). Any story

can be sequenced by placing pictures of representing stages of the story in order. Sequencing members of a family helps to give children a real idea of time. They need to know the order of child – parents – grandparents, and 'when Granny was a little girl' is much more easily understood than talking about 'years ago'. Victorian times might be described as 'when your great-great-great granny was a girl'. By the end of Key Stage 1, timelines should be used to sequence the periods of history that children have visited through stories and longer topics.

2 Knowledge and understanding of events, people and changes in the past

Many stories told to children of this age group demonstrate clear causation which they can understand and explain: 'Goldilocks chose Baby Bear's porridge because it was neither too hot nor too cold'; 'Because Bessie Coleman was the first black woman pilot, black pilots drop flowers on her grave'. Children must *recognise* the reasons rather than suggest reasons themselves, but many Key Stage 1 children are perfectly capable of doing both.

As we use stories set in the past it is important to emphasise the range of period detail that exists. Much of this detail will relate to domestic areas familiar to the children that can be readily compared with their own lives. Clothes, food, houses streets, music, toys and school are all good topics but you *can* also introduce unfamiliar things like castles and cannons and sailing ships that children will often find exotic and exciting. Showing pictures in story books and talking about them is a good opportunity for this sort of work. Role-play in a prepared home corner is an excellent way of exploring different ways of life – this will lay important groundwork for later history work.

3 Historical interpretation

Many teachers find identifying different ways in which the past is represented confusing. It is all about ways in which we, in the present, portray past events and people for our present purposes. Two stories about a Victorian childhood can present very different pictures of that period because they select different aspects to include, because they use different sources of information and simply because the writers have different opinions about the Victorians.

Children need to understand that the people writing the stories and films and creating the museum displays had to find out about the past from original sources. You might talk about illustrations in a story book and show how the illustrator must have used old photographs to find out about how to draw the costumes. You might talk about how the curator decided what things to put in a museum display and what to put on the labels. Many Key Stage 1 children, however, are quite capable of moving on to discuss why the selections and interpretations were made.

4 Historical enquiry

It is this element that points up the difference between history and fiction. History really happened and we find out about it by looking for evidence, clues from the past. Those who hated history at school usually did so because it was presented as a lot of dry facts which had to be memorised rather than an exciting piece of detective work. In Key Stage 1, teachers can both teach the concept of historical enquiry and lay a foundation of enquiry skills using different sorts of evidence.

Local history

The local environment is an essential source of historical evidence. Resources are rich, varied and available but often you need to find and prepare them yourself for the children's use. Whilst it is fascinating for children to use copies of sources, or even the originals themselves, many will need to be transcribed or modified for younger children to use. It is important to develop your own knowledge of the local area and the possibilities that it holds for study. It is also important to find out about local history records and archives and how to access the information they contain. The local history library or County Record Office is the first and best source of material, and the local history librarian will be your guide to its treasures.

Finding out about the past from a range of sources

Sources are sometimes divided into primary sources and secondary sources. Primary ones are 'firsthand evidence', material actually from the time being studied – old photographs, for instance. Secondary sources are created later than the time they describe, like historical novels, history books or computer simulations. Primary sources like old photographs and artefacts have a patina of age and they help children understand that history is about things that actually happened. Different sorts of sources need to be introduced and the children taught to use them.

● *Eyewitness accounts:* In the context of the infant classroom this will often mean adults talking about their own pasts but it can include firsthand accounts recorded in writing. Oral history is especially useful because it helps to make history real and believable by creating a direct link with it through a real person. Recording an interview is always advisable because you can then refer back to it and use it as a text. The most important skills for the children to learn are listening skills, and playing back a tape later can help them to practise them.

● *Pictures:* It is usually quite easy to find plenty of large format books in a public library containing old photographs of domestic life or children's lives in the past. Postcard-sized reproductions of old portraits are helpful and the English Heritage *Teacher's Guide to Using Portraits* is a useful publication. Local history libraries should have plenty of old pictures of the locality.

● *Artefacts:* An artefact is anything made by human hands. Old things allow us to touch the past and help us to imagine those past people who held the object before us. For young children, big objects that can be manipulated and used are best. It is not too difficult to find an old washboard and other washday paraphernalia, and actually using the objects will present and answer questions about people's lives in the past. Using slates and slate pencils might be another example.

● *Museums, buildings and archaeological sites:* Generally children will respond much better and achieve more if they understand that they are going on a trip to find answers from evidence. This means that the best time for the trip is often a little way into the topic, when the children are already involved and have formulated questions they want answered. The activities they engage in at the museum, building or site should involve really looking at and thinking about the evidence. To do this the children must be able to see clearly and spend at least ten or fifteen minutes concentrating on each exhibit or display.

Think about the questions that you will use to focus the children's investigation. It is important to encourage them to justify their answers, for example *Why do you think that? How do you know that?* rather than just asking for pieces of information. If it is allowed, use a camera to record different aspects of a visit. Recording answers and impressions on a cassette for later processing maximises valuable time.

5 Organisation and communication

Increasingly, you should be looking for coherent written work that deals with historical issues and questions. The QCA booklet 'Expectations in History' is very helpful in giving an idea of the average expected from each year group. Children need to learn to choose pieces of historical information to include in their story or picture or role-play. If they are drawing themselves in an Edwardian seaside scene, for example, they can include elements from Rosie's story (see page 122) or from old photographs. They must learn not to include anachronistic things like baseball caps. The communication skills involved are generic ones and their development should often be guided by the National Literacy Strategy (see 'History and literacy' overleaf).

Breadth of study

During Key Stage 1, children have to practise their knowledge, skills and understanding whilst studying four areas. These areas of study are not units as such, but they indicate the appropriate subject material to use whilst developing children's historical abilities. This book gives choices of

units using alternative content that provide roughly similar work in skills and understanding. Your choices may depend on supplementary material available in the local area, on the children's interests or your own enthusiasms and knowledge.

Cross-curricular links

History has natural links with many other areas of the curriculum and the planning grids in this book provide examples of where specific links can be made. However, it is worth detailing some of the areas of the curriculum where ties with history are particularly strong or important.

History and literacy

While the focus of a Literacy Hour should be literacy, the use of historical texts can enhance it. Such texts may have interesting uses of vocabulary, tenses or reported speech. Texts of all types can be found: fiction, non-fiction, letters, poems and so on. If a suitable text is used in a morning's Literacy Hour, later, in history time, the children have as a starting point a well-understood story. It is for this reason that some texts have been provided in this book.

History and ICT

History and ICT also have much to offer one another but individual activities may not have equal 'pay off' in each subject. Sometimes those applications that are most useful in promoting good history do not develop the child's ICT skills very much and vice versa. It is important therefore to be clear in your learning intentions as to whether the activity is primarily history or ICT.

● *Word processing and desktop publishing:* These applications are obviously invaluable to history. This will mainly be in connection with organising and communicating the children's knowledge of history, for example making history books, labels for wall displays, historical newspapers as well as straightforward pieces of writing.

● *Databases and datafiles:* Database work with programs like *Information Workshop* is desirable. Children could make data cards, including information gathered about historical figures or places. More modern software will allow pictures to be included. There are also prepared datafiles on CD-ROMs and encyclopaedias.

● *Timelines:* There are one or two packages available that operate in the same way as a timeline on a wall, except that it scrolls across the screen. Children can enter material, and on the more modern ones they can scan in photographs and so on. Information gained in topics can be entered and accumulated on the class timeline program. It should not replace the wall-mounted timeline, however, which has the advantage of being visible at all times.

● *Multimedia:* Packages like *Hyperstudio* probably offer the most exciting way forward because they allow the teacher and sometimes the child to create their own ICT resources. The basic model is of a stack of blank 'cards' on which text or pictures can be placed.

● *The Internet:* There is a growing body of information now on the Internet, including a large number of original historical documents. Many lesson plans in this book give relevant websites. You should always check websites yourself before allowing the children to access them as some are more suitable and easier to use than others.

History and citizenship/PSHE

Part of citizenship/PSHE involves children in 'learning to understand and respect our common humanity, diversity and differences'. History allows us to develop this understanding in a number of ways. It allows us to view the rich diversity of human experience over different periods of time. By investigating events in the past, children can consider social and moral dilemmas and question people's emotions and motivations and also consider the consequences of choices made. In investigating historical characters children can discuss the rights and wrongs of their actions.

Famous people

The National Curriculum specifies that children must find out about 'men, women and children' – it is a truism to say that women have largely been ignored in history. The priorities for learning in citizenship at Key Stage 1 include emphasis on recognising what is fair and unfair and respecting the differences between people.

The 'pioneering women' in the first unit of this chapter were all campaigners, in their own ways, against unfairness and discrimination. Discussion of their lives gives a context for debate about the contributions that men and women make to society. These women all lived between the mid-19th and early 20th centuries, and they represent the efforts of women to take their part in a man's world. The stories that are included as photocopiable pages have biographical content and they are intended to have a moral.

The 'men of their time' are, on the whole, more traditional and well-known choices. Leonardo da Vinci is included as the archetypal man of the Renaissance. He was a great investigator, observer and artist at a time when these qualities were transforming Europe. Francis Drake was a self-confident and courageous but perhaps rather amoral adventurer of the 'Age of Discovery', when Europe began to explore and exploit the world. Samuel Pepys is chosen because he was a spectator to the Great Fire. William Hogarth is a slightly more unusual selection, but his prints are a very accessible way for children to explore his age. As in the novels of his contemporaries Daniel Defoe and Henry Fielding, his works show very human characters in a bustling, exciting and rather dangerous world. Isambard Kingdom Brunel represents the Victorian 'can do' spirit that changed the physical character of the country. Nelson Mandela is a politician in a very political age. There is one man from each century from the 15th to the 20th. The characters are, in some fashion, representative of the spirit of their age. The choice of two artists among them may seem excessive, but it may be defended by the fact that artists are observers of their times. Their pictures also provide excellent source material that is easy for young children to access.

The overarching theme of this chapter is that of *story*. It is at the heart of history teaching as it has been at the heart of children's learning throughout history. Interest in people's lives is a fairly basic human characteristic and a love of history is usually engendered by delight in such tales. All the stories can be photocopied onto acetates and used with an overhead projector in the Literacy Hour.

The coming of the Literacy Hour has transformed the primary school curriculum. If the foundation subjects are to enjoy proper emphasis it can only be by forming a symbiotic relationship with the core ones. Literacy and history are natural bedfellows. History is nothing without story and story is nothing without a context. Much textual analysis requires skills identical to those necessary for the study of history. Through the context of history, children can sequence stories, identify and discuss reasons for events, discuss story settings, identify and describe characters, retell stories individually and through role-play as well as understanding the distinction between fact and fiction and scanning text for answers to questions. All these are required Literacy Hour tasks for Year 2.

Curriculum 2000 lays emphasis on the development of thinking skills such as information processing, reasoning, enquiry, creative thinking and evaluation. All these can be developed through the medium of the historical story. History and literacy can complement each other while still proving true to their own lines of development. When a historical text is used for the development of literacy, the child is given a clear purpose for decoding and understanding language. Subsequently the concentrated study of a complex text provides a rich historical resource.

Pioneering women

Enquiry questions	Learning objectives	Teaching activities	Learning outcomes	Literacy links	Cross-curricular links
Why did Bessie Coleman go to France?	● Give reasons for people in the past acting as they did.	Investigate story of Bessie Coleman and look at the work of pioneers of flight. Consider why Bessie had to go to France to qualify as a pilot.	Children: ● give reasons why Bessie wanted to fly and why she had to go to France to learn	Use the story sheet as a basis for shared poetry writing entitled 'The Air Show' or 'Bessie's Flight'.	Citizenship: consider social and moral dilemmas, look at questions of fairness and right and wrong. Science / design and technology: look at how propellers work and investigate aerodynamics and flight, such as gliders.
Why was the underground railway important?	● Find answers from sources that go beyond simple observations to make deductions.	Find out about the exploits of Harriet Tubman and how she contributed to the revolt against slavery.	● use the different sources to make deductions about Harriet's life	Compare different versions of Harriet's story by different authors. Look for points of similarity, points of difference and any questions that children would like to find out about. Use the story sheet as a basis for shared writing; continue the story to make a class or group book.	Numeracy: calculate distances. How long would it take on foot? How long would it take today? Geography: develop mapping skills through planning route. RE: find out about the story of Moses, investigate links. Music: look at negro spirituals. Drama: role play 'Escape on the Underground Railway'. Citizenship: identify and respect differences and similarities between people.
What did Mary Anning discover?	● Know that there are different ways in which the past can be represented.	Investigate the contribution of Mary Anning to the field of palaeontology. What did she discover?	● suggest how and why there are different versions of the story	Use reference books to research different types of dinosaurs and fossils.	Science: theory of evolution; look at scientific enquiry used to make sense of evidence of dinosaur bones.

Enquiry questions	Learning objectives	Teaching activities	Learning outcomes	Literacy links	Cross-curricular links
What did Elizabeth Fry do with her life?	● Use terms concerned with the passing of time and order events. ● Demonstrate factual knowledge and understanding of aspects of the past beyond living memory and of main events and people.	Investigate what being a Quaker meant to Elizabeth Fry and how she came to influence conditions in women's prisons.	● explain how and why Elizabeth Fry tried to help women prisoners ● order events from Elizabeth's life	Use the story sheet as a basis for play writing – turn a scene into a play for a class assembly. Shared writing of a factual account of conditions in Newgate Prison in the form of an official report.	RE: find out about the Religious Society of Friends or Quakers. Research other prominent Quakers and arrange visit if possible. Design and technology: textiles – look at patchwork quilts, research some traditional patterns, make simple class patchwork; invite in an enthusiast to demonstrate techniques.
How has medicine changed since Elizabeth Garrett Anderson became a doctor?	● Make distinctions between aspects of their own lives and those of other times.	Compare modern medicine with that of the late Victorian period. Look at the developments in medical techniques.	● recognise differences between Victorian medicine and that of the present	Use simple references including an index and a glossary to find out specific information. Make a class glossary of different terms linked to the unit.	Science: realise the contribution that science made to the development of medicine. Citizenship: discuss the treatment of women who wanted to be doctors – was it fair?
What did Margaret Macdonald Mackintosh do?	● Recognise characteristic features of a period/ movement.	Look at the work of Margaret Macdonald Mackintosh and understand how it was representative of the 'Glasgow Style'.	● recognise elements of Margaret's work and explain how it relates to a certain style.	Listen to traditional Scottish folk tales. Retell, rewrite and illustrate with Macdonald type drawings.	Art: paintings in the style of Charles Rennie Mackintosh and Margaret Macdonald Mackintosh using watercolour washes.

Pioneering
women

① Why did Bessie Coleman go to France?

Background information

Although people have dreamed of flying with the birds since the beginning of time, the story of flight really begins in the 20th century. In 1903 Wilber and Orville Wright achieved the first powered flight. In 1909 Louis Blériot flew a monoplane across the Channel for the first time. By 1914 aircraft could regularly be seen in the skies of Europe and North America. The First World War led to huge technological advances in early aviation. By 1919 a transatlantic flight was made by John Alcock and Arthur Whitten-Brown, to be followed by Charles Lindbergh flying solo in 1927. The air was not the sole province of men, however, and from the very beginning women were also enthralled by the prospect of fight. Hilda Hewitt and Harriet Quimbley were keen to involve themselves with this new adventure. These early pioneers were followed by Amelia Earhart and Amy Johnson. Bessie Coleman was one of those who were active in the Twenties and Thirties in opening up this exciting new form of transport.

Bessie Coleman was born on 26 January 1893 in Atlanta, Texas. She grew up in a small farming community after her father, a Cherokee Indian, returned to his traditional lands in Oklahoma. Bessie's mother was a strong-willed and stubborn woman, determined that her children should escape the grinding poverty of the cotton fields. She urged Bessie to 'become somebody' and encouraged her to learn to read. Bessie later said, '…I found a brand new world through the written word. I couldn't get enough.' It was through reading newspaper reports of the First World War that Bessie became interested in flying. She soon came to realise, however, that 'no one had ever heard of a black woman pilot in 1919'. Bessie refused to take no for an answer but eventually discovered that if she wanted to fly she would have to cross the ocean to France to learn. After saving up enough money for her journey and learning French at night school, Bessie set off for Paris.

On 15 June 1921 Bessie became the first black woman in the world to gain her pilot's licence. 'I did it,' she said. 'I got above those cotton fields!' Bessie learned to perform stunts and aerobatics and became a renowned barnstormer. She put on daring air displays all over America. The crowds, both black and white, loved her and called her 'Brave Bessie'. She was determined to save enough money to set up her own flying school that would make it easier for black peple to become pilots.

Early aviation was a dangerous business, however, and tragically on 30 April 1926 Bessie's plane flipped over and she fell to her death. Although Bessie couldn't open her school her example inspired others to do so. Every year, on the anniversary of her death, black pilots drop flowers on her grave.

Bessie explained her need to fly when she said that, 'The sky is the only place where there is no prejudice. Up there everyone is equal. Everyone is free.'

What you need and preparation

Make a timeline of flight, using information found in reference books. You will also need: *Nobody Owns the Sky* by Reeve Lindbergh (Walker Books) – optional; a picture of a biplane; an A1 sheet of paper with a picture of Bessie Coleman in the centre; photocopiable page 101; paper; writing and drawing materials.

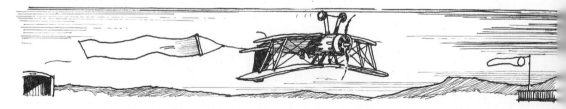

What to do

(30 mins) Introduction

Introduce the subject of flight and ask the children about any experiences of flying that they have had:

● Where did you go?

● Did you enjoy it?

● What sort of things do you remember?

Pick up any possible stereotypes that arise in the discussion, such as female – stewardess, male – pilot. Using the timeline of British history, ask the children how long they think people have been flying. Alternatively, help them by suggesting some famous people that they may know and ask them if those people could have flown.

Now look at the timeline of flight in more detail. Run though the dates and explain who the main characters were. Point out that many of them were quite young. (Ensure that the children know that not all the important people in the history of flight have been included.) Explain that each of these people was a pioneer. Ask:

● What does this mean?

● Why do you think people wanted to do such things, especially when so many of them lost their lives doing so?

Tell the story of one of these pioneers – Bessie Coleman (see 'Background information' and the book *Nobody Owns the Sky*, if you have a copy), and read aloud 'The air show' on photocopiable page 101. Ask the children:

● Was Bessie's family rich or poor, and how do we know? Why didn't Bessie go to college?

● What was her job? Where did she go to learn to fly? What did she do when she returned and why did she do this?

Discuss with the children why Bessie had to go to Paris and why she could not become a pilot in America. What do they think about this?

Show the children a picture of a biplane like Bessie's and discuss what it may have been like to fly in it. Does it look like a plane of today? How was it powered and what was it made of?

Look at the picture of Bessie. What impression does it give? What sort of person do the children think she was? Give some of Bessie's own reasons for why she flew and explain what she was trying to achieve. Tell the children about the annual ceremony in which black pilots drop flowers on Bessie's grave.

(20 mins) Development

Ask the children to storyboard three or more scenes from Bessie's life, in sequence, and then complete the statement: *Bessie wanted to fly because...*

(10 mins) Plenary

Ask the children for their final thoughts on Bessie's story. Write some of their comments around the picture of Bessie on the A1 sheet of paper. This can be used as a poster for display.

Differentiation

Provide adult support for less able children and instead of asking them to produce a storyboard, invite them to suggest three things they have found out about Bessie's life and illustrate them. More able children could write and illustrate an account of Bessie's life, including reasons why they think she wanted to do such things.

Assessing learning outcomes

Can the children give reasons why Bessie wanted to fly and why she had to go to France to learn?

ICT opportunities

Use the Internet to research more about early pioneers of flight.

Follow-up activities

● Put Bessie's story into the wider picture of the history of flight. Link it with the local area, if possible – were there any local industries or people connected with flight?

● Find out further information about 'firsts', for example powered flight, transatlantic flight. Look at how early pioneers influenced those who came later.

● Look at later elements of the story (the Battle of Britain and Douglas Bader, Tuskagee Airmen, the development of commercial flight) and bring the story up to date, including an exploration of space.

● Arrange a visit to an airport to look at modern planes.

Pioneering women

(1 hour) Why was the underground railway important?

Learning objective
Find answers from sources that go beyond simple observations to make deductions.

Lesson organisation
Teacher-led discussion; group investigation; group and individual work.

Vocabulary
underground
railway
slavery
escape
plantation
Quakers
abolitionist

Background information

The southern states of America at the turn of the 19th century were economically reliant on the labour of black slaves. Many people, especially Quakers, felt slavery was wrong and were prepared to help runaway slaves. They set up a system of safe houses and provided guides to help the escaped slaves. This network was known as the 'Underground Railway'. The escaping slaves were known as 'passengers', the safe houses were called 'stations' and children were 'parcels'. Escaping slaves could expect to be hunted at every step of the way.

Harriet Tubman was born a slave around 1820 on a cotton plantation in Bucktown, Maryland in the southern states of America. Harriet was always determined to escape, and in 1849 she made the journey north to freedom. Not content just to remain safely where she was, Harriet returned 19 times and brought over 300 people to freedom. She worked as a conductor on the underground railway – the network of safe houses that stretched from the deep south through the northern states to Canada.

Harriet planned her escapes meticulously and was daring and fearless. She was so successful that at one time she had a price of $40 000 on her head. She was proud to be able to say, 'I never ran my train off the track and I never lost a passenger'. Included in those passengers were her own parents and all her brothers and sisters. During the Civil War, Harriet served as a nurse and then a spy. She also led Union soldiers in raids into the Confederate states. Towards the end of her long life, Harriet opened a home for old, homeless ex-slaves, where she herself lived until she died.

She died on 10 March 1913 in Auburn, New York. Throughout her life Harriet never forgot the moment when she realised she was free: 'I looked at my hands to see if I was the same person now I was free. There was such glory through the trees and over the fields, and I felt like I was in heaven.'

More information can be found on: www.brightmoments.com/blackhistory/nhtubman.html; www.camalott.com/~rssmith/Moses.html; and in the book *History Makers of the Industrial Revolution* by Nigel Smith (Wayland).

What you need and preparation

Obtain a copy of *Aunt Harriet's Underground Railroad in the Sky* by Faith Ringgold (Crown Publishers), if possible. Compile a pack of information for each group about Harriet Tubman's life and her achievements (include a photograph of Harriet and maps of the general area in addition to factual information about Harriet – see 'Background information'). Prepare a sketch map of Harriet's escape route and draw and cut out a small figure of Harriet. You will also need: a map of the southern states; a set of coloured spots (three-quarters of one colour and one quarter of another); board or flip chart; writing materials.

What to do

(25 mins) Introduction

As the children come into the classroom, give them a coloured spot. Now sort the children into two sets according to the spot that they have been given. Inform them that the smaller set is now in charge of the larger, and this set must do everything that the smaller set tells them to do. Allow one of the children from the small set to be a caller for a 'Simon Says' type game. The small group can join in if they want to, but the large group must do everything they are told to do. Ask the children whether they feel that this is a fair system. What do the children in the small group think? What about the children in the large group? Tell the children that there have been many different periods in history in which human beings have treated each other badly.

Explain that you are going to tell the story of one of those times and one of the people who tried to change things. Tell the children the story of Harriet Tubman (see 'Background information' and the book *Aunt Harriet's Underground Railroad in the Sky*, if you have a copy). Move the figure of Harriet along the sketch map as the different places on her journey are reached. Ask the children:

- What was Harriet trying to do? Why did she have to do this? Why did people help her?
- What did Harriet feel like when she reached Pennsylvania ? How far did she have to travel?

Mary travelled from Bucktown, Virginia, through Middleton, Maryland and Newcastle, Wilmington and Camden in Delaware until she reached Philadelphia in Pennsylvania. The distance was 90 miles. Later Harriet had to get slaves to St Catherine's near Niagra Falls in Canada. This was much further, at 500 miles.

Finish this part of the session by reading the story 'The Moses of her people' on photocopiable page 102.

Follow-up activities
●Individually, the children can fill in a map to show Harriet's journey.
●Look at the work of other abolitionists on both sides of the Atlantic, including people such as William Wilberforce and Equiano Obodiah.

(20 mins) Development

Put the children into groups and give out your prepared packs of information on Harriet Tubman. Ask the children to work together to answer the following questions about what happened to Harriet after her escape:

- What did Harriet do after she escaped? Write down three things that you found out about her.
- Why did the plantations offer a reward for Harriet's capture?
- Why was Harriet called 'the Moses of her people'?
- What would it have been like to travel on the underground railway? Why do you think this?

(15 mins) Plenary

Ask each group to give feedback to the rest of the class about what they now know about Harriet Tubman. Invite one or two of the children to say what they think the underground railway was and why they think it was important.

ICT
Use the Internet to find further information about Harriet Tubman and other abolitionists such as Sojourner Truth.

Differentiation
Differentiate the information provided in the packs and provide adult support for less able children.

Assessing learning outcomes
Can the children use the different sources to make deductions about Harriet's life?

(1 hour) What did Mary Anning discover?

Background information
Palaeontology or the study of fossils is a relatively new discipline. Although fossils had been found in the past it wasn't until the 19th century that people began to study their finds and examine the bones of these long-dead creatures buried deep in the rocks. The curio collectors of the early Victorian period gathered and displayed these unusual finds. The study of specimens such as these helped Charles Darwin develop his theory of evolution. Much valuable work collecting and categorising samples was completed by enthusiastic amateurs or self-taught experts such as Mary Anning.

Mary Anning was born in Lyme Regis, Dorset on 21 May 1799. Her father Richard was a cabinet maker by trade and also a keen amateur fossil collector. When Mary was only 11, however, her father died leaving the family almost destitute. The only income the family possessed were the wages of Joseph, Mary's brother, a trainee upholsterer. Luckily Mary's father had passed on his skills and enthusiasm for finding 'curiosities' to both his children. The cliffs around the town

Learning objective
Know that there are different ways in which the past can be represented.

Lesson organisation
Pairs activity; teacher-led discussion; group development and whole-class plenary.

Pioneering women

Vocabulary
palaeontology
geology
fossil
specimen
curios
theory
collect
categorise
dinosaur
ancient creatures
discover
ammonite
museum

ICT opportunities
Research palaeontology further by logging onto a museum site such as the Natural History Museum or the British Museum.

provided a fertile hunting ground for Mary. She set herself up in business, selling her finds to local enthusiasts and passing tourists. She was particularly supported by Lt Col Birch, another amateur fossil collector, who helped raise money for the family by auctioning his own personal collection of fossils.

When Mary was only about 12, she and her brother discovered the first specimen of an Ichthyosaurus, which she sold for the princely sum of £23. Later on she unearthed her most spectacular find, which was a Plesiosaur from the Jurassic period. This time Mary found the creature herself with only the help of her little black and white dog. Mary died where she had been born, in Lyme Regis on 9 March 1847.

Mary was a poor girl with little formal education. Through hard work and determination she became a legitimate and respected 'fossilist' providing many fine specimens for the scientific community. Although self-educated, Mary became so knowledgeable that her opinion was sought by many eminent scientists and collectors. Her contribution to the study of palaeontology is largely overlooked, partly because of her gender and the time in which she lived. She was well respected in her own time, however. As Lady Harriet Silvester noted in 1824: '…by reading and application she has arrived to that degree of knowledge as to be in the habit of writing and talking with professors and other clever men on the subject, and they all acknowledge that she understands more of the science than anyone else in the kingdom.'

More information can be found on: www.sdsc.edu/ScienceWomen/anning.html; ww.ucmp.berkeley.edu/history/anning.html; www.turnpike.net/~mscott/anning.html; www.turnpike.net/~mscott/women.html; and in the book *Mary Anning's Treasures* by Helen Bush (Heinemann Educational).

What you need and preparation

Collect together some pictures of dinosaur skeletons, enough for one between two children; cut up each picture to make a jigsaw (make some jigsaws very simple and others a little more complicated). Find some reference books on dinosaurs and fossils. You will also need: information about Mary Anning from textbooks and the Internet; a map showing Lyme Regis; a picture of Mary Anning and her discoveries; photocopiable page 103; *Stone Girl Bone Girl* by Laurence Anholt (Picture Corgi) – optional; board or flip chart; writing materials.

What to do

30 mins Introduction

Give each pair of children a dinosaur jigsaw and ask them to try to put the pieces back together. Don't tell them at this stage what the completed jigsaw will show. After allowing the children a few minutes to try to complete the task, ask:

● How well did you manage to fit the pieces together?

● What made it difficult or easy? Were some jigsaws simpler than others?

● Were you able to work out what the jigsaw showed?

Now talk about how the study of fossils is like putting tiny jigsaw pieces from the past back together and read the children the story of Mary Anning (see 'Background information' and the book *Stone Girl Bone Girl*, if you have a copy). Read the story 'She sells seashells on the sea shore' on photocopiable page 103.

Discuss the main points of the story by asking the children:

● Where did Mary live?

● Was her family rich or poor? How do you know this?

● What did Mary do with her curiosities? Why do you think she did this?

● What do you think Mary discovered on the beach?

Collate their answers on the board and any additional information that arises.

Pioneering
women

(20 mins) Development

Help the children to research Mary's life by looking at the factual information in the textbooks together. They can then compare their findings with the answers they gave to your questions following the story. Ask the children to make notes in groups. How close is the story to Mary's life? Are there any differences between the story version and the facts? Which version is correct?

(10 mins) Plenary

Record on the board some of the results of the group discussions, and encourage the children to justify their choices.

Differentiation

As the development work is a challenging activity, it is important to provide adult support for lower- ability groups.

Assessing learning outcomes

Can the children suggest how and why there are different versions of the same story?

Follow-up activities

● Teach the children 'She sells seashells on the sea shore' and ask them to illustrate the tongue-twister for a class display.
● Research the history of scientific development, and look at some of the major scientific discoveries. Investigate the people who were instrumental in promoting the ideas or making the discoveries.

(1 hour) What did Elizabeth Fry do with her life?

Background information

Britain at the beginning of the 19th century was a mixture of great wealth on the one hand and extreme poverty and squalor on the other. Those with money were isolated from and sometimes completely unaware of the grinding misery of the poor living just outside their doors. War with France had damaged the economy. Bread prices were soaring and people were literally starving in the streets, especially in the big cities. This inevitably led to a massive increase of crime. There were stricter and stricter punishments imposed by the authorities. There were over two hundred crimes that were punishable by death and thousands were transported to the colonies, mainly Australia. Newgate prison in London was one of the most notorious. Few people wanted to know what went on in the prisons, let alone try to change them.

Elizabeth Fry was born on 21 May 1780, the third child of Joseph and Catherine Gurney, a family of wealthy Quaker merchants. Elizabeth, or Betsy as the family called her, had a privileged upbringing, playing with her brothers and sisters in the big house in the country near Norwich. Betsy's mother thought that girls as well as boys should be educated, and so Betsy was taught subjects that most other girls weren't, such as history and Latin. The Gurneys were not strict Quakers and the behaviour of the family sometimes shocked their plain Quaker neighbours. When Betsy was 18 she heard a famous American Quaker, William Savery, speak. He changed the direction of Elizabeth's life as she felt she had begun to understand her religion. Elizabeth began to become more involved with the poor, helping set up a little Bible school for underprivileged children.

In August 1800 Elizabeth married Joseph Fry, with whom she had eleven children. Although Elizabeth spent much time managing her large family she still found time for her charitable work. In 1812 she visited Newgate prison for the first time. What she found shocked her and she was determined to try to help. Elizabeth was very practical and organised schools for the children and useful occupation for the women. She comforted condemned women before their execution. She visited more than 100 convict ships before they sailed for Australia with transported convicts.

Elizabeth also ran soup kitchens for the poor, set up schools and established a training school for nurses. She travelled up and down the countryside advocating various reforms. She was one of the most well known women of her time. When she died on 12 October 1845, hundreds came to stand at her funeral as she was buried in the Quaker burial ground at Barking, Essex.

Learning objective
● Use terms concerned with the passing of time and order events.
● Demonstrate factual knowledge and understanding of aspects of the past beyond living memory and of main events and people.

Lesson organisation
Whole-class teacher-led discussion; group role play.

Vocabulary
prison
gaol
turnkey
transportation
prisoner
execution
reformer
quaker
patchwork
fetters

CHAPTER 1
FAMOUS PEOPLE

Pioneering women

More information can be found on: www.quaker.org.uk/qviews3.html; and in the books *Elizabeth Fry* by Angela Bull (Hamish Hamilton); *Friend of Prisoners, the Story of Elizabeth Fry* by Geoffrey Hanks (Religious & Moral Education Press); *Elizabeth Fry and Prison Reform* by David Johnson (Jackdaw Publications); *Victorians* by Clare Chandler (Wayland).

What you need and preparation
Find a portrait of Elizabeth Fry (see above for sources) and a plan of Newgate prison (see *Friend of Prisoners, the Story of Elizabeth Fry* and *Elizabeth Fry and Prison Reform*) – optional. You will also need: a map of the world; photocopiable page 104; board or flip chart; a large sheet of paper.

What to do
25 mins **Introduction**
Show the children the portrait of Elizabeth Fry. Do not tell them who the person is at this stage, just try to draw out their initial thoughts:
● What impression do you have of this person?
● What do you think she was like?
Collate the children's answers on the board, ensuring that they try to justify their answers, for example *I think she was… because…*

Tell the children that you are going to read them a story about this person and ask if they can listen carefully to find out her name. Read 'The Maria sets sail' on photocopiable page 104.
Following the story, ask the children:
● What do you think was happening?
● Why do you think the women were in chains?
● Where might they have been going?
● Now who do you think the woman in the picture is and why do you think this?

Explain the idea of transportation. Look at a world map and point out the route taken (London; Rio de Janeiro; Cape Town; Indian Ocean; Botany Bay, Australia), telling the children that it was a journey of four or five months. Explain what sort of thing happened at the end of the journey. Try to get the children to imagine what it would have been like and how the convicts would have felt so far from home with everything so very different. Consider, for example, how strange creatures like kangaroos must have looked if you had never seen one before, and help the children to think about important questions such as:
● Would the convicts ever return to Britain?
● What was it like for the children?
● What had the women done to deserve this sort of punishment?

Tell the children about the other things that Elizabeth Fry had done with her life – how she had tried to help the poor through setting up schools and soup kitchens – but explain that she is chiefly remembered for her prison reforms. Talk about conditions in Newgate prison at the time, using the plan of the prison, if you have one, to help children to visualise what it was like. Tell them how Elizabeth set about changing things, and finish with the question: *Why did she want to do this?*

20 mins **Development**
Split the children into three groups. Work with one group at a time to produce a living picture or tableau showing a scene from Elizabeth's life, for example Elizabeth helping convicts onto the prison ships, Elizabeth visiting the women in Newgate prison, Elizabeth watching *The Maria* set sail. Give each of the children a character and a set position for their initial 'freeze', then tell them to let their freezes come to life. Encourage them to think of a short line of dialogue that their character might say. Make sure that the children say their lines in sequence, as you visit each group.

 Plenary
15 mins
Ask each group to perform their tableau and short scene to the rest of the class.
Return to the portrait of Elizabeth Fry and the children's comments that you wrote on the board at the beginning of the session. Ask the children if there is anything that they wish to change or add. Write down any further statements that the children offer and display them on a large sheet of paper next to the portrait of Elizabeth Fry.

Differentiation
Ask more able children to draw one of the reforms that Elizabeth tried to make and to complete the statement: *Elizabeth Fry tried to change things because…*

Assessing learning outcomes
Can the children explain how and why Elizabeth Fry tried to help women prisoners? Can they sequence episodes from Elizabeth's life?

Follow-up activity
Find out about modern societies that work to encourage better social conditions and look at the continuing work of Barnardo's and the Salvation Army.

How has medicine changed since Elizabeth Garrett Anderson became a doctor?
1 hour 10 mins

Background information
The Victorian era saw tremendous advances in the field of medicine and public health. The great teaching hospitals were more efficiently organised and doctors flocked to attend the big medical schools. The horrors of the Crimean War led to changes in the way that hospitals were organised and run. Florence Nightingale established her School of Nursing linked to St Thomas's Hospital, London. Anaesthetics and antiseptics were discovered and made treatment more effective. Queen Victoria was the first British monarch to have an anaesthetic, during the birth of her eighth child. The link between germs and infection became known and improved sanitation and public water supplies led to better public health. Although medical schools on the continent were prepared to allow woman to sit degrees and become doctors, this was not considered a suitable profession for a women in Britain.

Further information can be found in *Elizabeth Garrett Anderson* by Jo Martin (Methuen) and *British History, Imperial Britain* (Kingfisher), and on the website www.spartacus.schoolnet.co.uk/WandersonE.htm.

What you need and preparation
Collect together some pictures of Victorian hospitals and doctors (including one large picture) and modern hospitals and doctors. Find simple textbooks about Victorian hospitals, Florence Nightingale and Mary Seacole.

Arrange for someone from the medical profession to visit the children, perhaps a local doctor or a medical student. Ask them to bring with them equipment that they would use on a daily basis such as a stethoscope and thermometer. Ask the children to prepare some questions beforehand that they would like to ask the visitor (see below). You will also need: photocopiable pages 105 and 106; tape recorder; writing materials.

What to do
30 mins **Introduction**
Ask the children what they know about doctors:
• What sort of doctors do they have themselves?
• Have they seen doctors in hospitals, on television programmes, in the news and so on?

Learning objective
Make distinctions between aspects of their own lives and those of other times.

Lesson organisation
Whole-class, discussion with visitor; whole-class, teacher-led discussion; individual follow up.

Vocabulary
doctor
medicine
training
medical school
hospital
ward
nurse
patient
apothecary
chemist

Pioneering women

Follow-up activities
● Study the ways in which women at this time fought for equality. Look at other pioneers such as Emily Davis (education), Emmeline and Christabel Pankhurst (votes for women), medicine (Sophia Jex Blake, Elsie Maud Inglis), travel (Mary Kingsley, Alexandra David Neel).
● Look at the history of medicine and the people who were influential in making changes: Louis Pasteur (pasteurisation), Edward Jenner and Lady Mary Montagu Wortley (inoculation), Charles Drew (creation of blood banks), Alexander Fleming (discovery of penicillin). Find out about the effect that these changes had on life for ordinary people, and link this to current medical advances and initiatives.

● Can anyone become a doctor?
● What do you need to do to become one?
  Introduce the speaker and let them explain their job and how they trained. Invite the children to put forward their questions, such as:
● Why did you want to be a doctor?
● How long did you have to train for, and did you go away to study?
● What sort of things did you have to learn?
● What happened when you qualified, and did you get a certificate?
● What sort of things have you done since you qualified?
  Encourage the children to try to find out as much as they can about the person and their job. Tape record the answers for later discussion.

(30 mins) Development
Show the children the large picture of the Victorian hospital scene. Ask them to explain what they can see. Can they suggest three words to describe the doctor in the picture? What impression does the picture give the children? Would they have liked to have gone to this hospital? Why do they think that?

Give the children some background to the changes that happened to medicine during the Victorian period: the development of anaesthetic (James Simpson, 1840s); the development of antiseptics (Joseph Lister, 1860s); the discovery of X-rays (Wilhelm Röntgen). Explain what the different advances were and encourage the children to think of how they contributed to better health care. Explain how people began to understand the link between dirt and disease, and help them to consider why this was important.

Talk about how women began to play a larger role in medicine in general, starting with the changes in nursing; refer to the work of Florence Nightingale and Mary Seacole. What about if a woman wanted to be a doctor, could she do this? Let the children tell you what they think, then explain how Elizabeth Garrett Anderson was rejected when she applied to study with a medical school, because she was a woman. What impression does this give the children? Do they think this is right or fair? Talk about how these women were pioneers (explain the meaning of *pioneer*).

Read the children the story of Elizabeth Garrett Anderson on photocopiable page 105. How do they think she managed to eventually work as a doctor? Give the children some background information (see sources above) and explain what Anderson did and what she wanted to achieve by starting the New Hospital for Women and Children.

Distribute copies of photocopiable page 106 and ask the children to look carefully at the pictures and identify differences between them.

(10 mins) Plenary
Working as a whole class, study the pictures of Victorian hospitals and those of modern ones. Challenge the children to identify as many differences as they can.

Differentiation
Ensure that less able children take part in the discussions.

Assessing learning outcomes
Can the children recognise differences between Victorian medicine and that of the present?

1 hour What did Margaret Macdonald Mackintosh do?

Background information

Glasgow School of Art at the end of the 19th century was an acknowledged leader in innovative design. Under the leadership of Francis 'Fra' Newberry the college flowered, and women were admitted as full and equal members. Four of the most influential students were the sisters Frances and Margaret Macdonald, Herbert McNair and Charles Rennie Mackintosh. They were a hugely talented group with eclectic interests, working in various areas including architecture, interior design, metalwork and graphic design. They formed mutually inspiring professional relationships that were to last for the rest of their lives. They were central to the development of the 'Glasgow Style'.

The aim of this activity is to recognise the artistic contribution of Margaret. More information can be found in *Glasgow Girls, Women in Art and Design 1880–1920*, edited by Jude Burkhauser (Canongate). There are numerous websites dedicated to Charles Rennnie Mackintosh and some also have information on Margaret: www.gla.ac.uk/Museum/ArtGall/artpub/p&p.html is the Hunterian Art Gallery, Glasgow and has examples of Margaret's work for sale through mail order.

What you need and preparation

Find some examples of Margaret Macdonald Mackintosh's work (see sources above) and of interior design by Charles and Margaret. You will also need: small magnifying glasses; prepared worksheet – see 'Development'; writing materials.

What to do

30 mins Introduction
Ask the children what they think of when people talk about 'art'. Ask them to draw or describe an artist, thinking about what sort of person an artist is.

Look at pictures of the tearooms and other rooms that Charles and Margaret designed. Point out some of the key features, such as the Glasgow Rose motif; colour schemes; strong vertical lines; swirling, rounded lines. Help the children to recognise what is meant by 'Glasgow Style.'

20 mins Development
Split the children into pairs or small groups, and give each pair or group an example of Margaret's work together with an analysis sheet that includes these sections: *The name of your painting and the date that it was completed. Do you like your painting, and why? Describe the painting in three words. What have you found that links with 'Glasgow Style'? Look closely at one of these features. Draw it and explain why you chose it.*

Provide magnifying glasses for the children to look at details. Ask them to answer the questions once they have discussed their findings.

10 mins Plenary
Invite each group to give feedback to the class. Did they like the painting? What words did they use to descibe it? How did it link to the 'Glasgow Style'? What feature did they draw?

Differentiation

Provide a simplified version of the analysis sheet for less able children and include some suggestions for statements that children might use.

Assessing learning outcomes

Can the children recognise elements of Margaret's work and explain how it relates to a certain style?

Learning objective
Recognise characteristic features of a period/movement.

Lesson organisation
Whole-class, teacher-led introduction; work in pairs or groups.

Vocabulary
art nouveau
Art and Crafts Movement
Glasgow Style
artist
motif
design
craft
architecture
interior design
printing
metalwork
embroidery
illustrations and graphic art
costume
watercolour
college
commission
patron
tearoom

Follow-up activities
● Ask each child to draw a Glasgow Rose, colour it in and write its name, copying the Mackintosh style script, to add to a class display.
● Build up a class reference book of women artists and share the information with the rest of the school in a class assembly.

Men of their time

Enquiry questions	Learning objectives	Teaching activities	Learning outcomes	Literacy links	Cross-curricular links
Who was Leonardo da Vinci?	● Identify differences between ways of life at different times. ● Find out about the past from a range of sources.	Read the story and discuss aspects of paintings by Leonardo looking at clothes, food etc.	Children: ● put correct aspects of Renaissance dress in their pictures		Art: investigate the work of Leonardo. Science: recognise and compare external parts of humans, animals and insects.
Who was Francis Drake?	● Sequence the voyage of *The Golden Hinde*. ● Give some reasons for Drake acting as he did.	Read the story and role-play the voyage. Sort arguments used by characters in the story.	● give reasons why Drake sailed around the world ● retell the story	Understand time and sequential relationships in stories. Use language to explore and convey situations, characters and emotions. Retell stories using knowledge of sequence and story language.	Geography: use geographical vocabulary like *north, south, east* and *west, ocean, near* and *far;* use globes and maps to follow a route.
Who was Samuel Pepys?	● Make interpretations of the past. ● Answer questions using certain sources. ● Place events in order.	Read the story and sequence the story using pictures.	● sequence the story ● answer simple questions about Pepys and the fire after listening to the story ● make some distinctions between the accounts (original extracts from Pepys and Evelyn)	Understand sequential events in stories. Write dialogue. Use language to explore and convey situations and characters. Recognise that non-fiction accounts can present similar information in different ways.	PSHE: talk about fire safety.

Enquiry questions	Learning objectives	Teaching activities	Learning outcomes	Literacy links	Cross-curricular links
Who was William Hogarth?	● Find answers from sources on the basis of simple observation or in ways that go beyond simple observation.	Read the story and use a Hogarth print to find out about 18th century London.	● find answers from the picture on the basis of simple observation or in ways that go beyond simple observation	Write sustained stories about what is going on in the print, using narrative, setting, characterisation and dialogue.	Music: Handel's *Water Music*. Art: printing, collagraphs.
Who was Isambard Kingdom Brunel?	● Give reasons why people in the past acted as they did.	Read the story and debate arguments for and against the railway.	● understand and give reasons for different opinions about the railways	Speech marks and their use in the speech bubbles.	Geography: railway maps.
Who is Nelson Mandela?	● Recognise why people did things and what happened as a result.	Read the story and give reasons for opinions about Mandela.	● give reasons for their opinions about Mandela.	Express own views using words and phrases from a text.	Citizenship: recognise what is fair and unfair, right and wrong.

(50 mins) Who was Leonardo da Vinci?

Learning objectives
● Identify differences between the way of life at different times.
● Find out about the past from a range of sources.

Lesson organisation
Teacher-led discussion with the whole class, group work.

Vocabulary
shield
apprentice
lizard

ICT opportunities
Use the Internet to carry out further research.

Follow-up activity
Ask the children to draw their own monsters, mixing up features of animals with those of insects.

Background information

Leonardo was the archetypal Renaissance figure. He was multi-talented, being a great painter, sculptor, architect and inventor. He was also a good musician and singer. The story on photocopiable page 107 is based on extracts from Giorgio Vasari's *Lives of the Artists*. Vasari was born in 1511, by which time Leonardo had gone to live in France, so he did not know him personally. However, Vasari did know many friends and contemporaries of Leonardo and incidents like his freeing of caged birds and the painting of the shield are certainly gathered from people with personal memories of the events. Unfortunately, the shield has not survived! The ending of the story may sound rather twee, but all contemporary accounts do seem to remark on what an extremely nice man Leonardo was. Having dwelt on the multifarious talents of the man we should not forget that kindness is also a very desirable quality in a hero.

What you need and preparation

Collect together some Renaissance pictures and drawings, reproduced to show to the class. Choose pictures that have clothing, scenery, architecture or food in them. One version of *The Annunciation* by Leonardo has an angel with wings copied from a bird; *The Last Supper* has a table full of food; *The Baptism of Christ* by Verrocchio has a small blond angel by young Leonardo. Books in the oversize section of your local library will provide examples. There are also plenty on the Internet; try www.artcyclopedia.com/artists/leonardo_da_vinci.html. You will also need: photocopiable page 107; paper; drawing materials.

What to do

(20 mins) Introduction

Read the story on the photocopiable sheet to the children. Then discuss some of the main points, highlighting Leonardo's interest in nature and the close observational drawing which was at the heart of Renaissance thinking.

Now show a reproduction of a Renaissance painting by Leonardo, or a contemporary, to the children. Discuss what is different about the clothes and other aspects, asking the children:
● What can you see?
● What is it about?
● What sort of clothes did people wear then? (Even in Biblical scenes Renaissance artists painted contemporary detail.)
● What were the houses like?
● What activities are going on?

(20 mins) Development

Split the children into groups, and give each group a reproduction of a Renaissance painting to use as reference. Ask the children to draw a picture of Leonardo in the story, giving him the right clothes, such as hose (leggings), a short doublet (jacket) and a suitable hat.

(10 mins) Plenary

Invite the children to show their drawings to the rest of the class. Discuss how similar they are to the reproductions, noting similarities and differences. Draw the children's attention to details that reflect people's way of life at the time.

Differentiation

Ask more able children to look at Leonardo's sketchbooks (available from the website mentioned previously) and try to explain what he was drawing.

Assessing learning outcomes

Can the children put correct aspects of Renaissance dress in their pictures?

Who was Francis Drake?

Background information

The events in the story on photocopiable page 108 take place in 1578. Spain at this time was the richest nation in Europe because it (with Portugal) controlled the whole of South and Central America. In particular, the silver mines of Peru sent a constant stream of wealth back to Spain via the 'silver fleet' that sailed in convoy from Panama City. Drake made a living by stealing this treasure. The morality of Drake's piracy might be a matter for debate as it was in his own time. He was a privateer, which meant that he had a licence from the queen to prey on enemy ships, and she herself profited a lot from this arrangement. On the other hand, Drake never bothered much whether England and Spain were at war or not at any particular moment. There was an element of personal vendetta over friends captured and executed by the Inquisition. As the story states, Drake was not wanton in his violence and, after a slaving expedition in his youth, he showed a marked distaste for slavery. He used escaped slaves (cimarrones or maroons) as allies on more than one occasion. Drake took part in (but did *not* command) the Armada fight; he sailed twice more to the Americas and died of tropical disease whilst leading an expedition in the West Indies in 1596. The Portuguese ship mentioned in the story was that of Ferdinand Magellan, which circumnavigated the world from west to east in 1521, though Magellan was killed on the way.

Learning objectives
● Sequence the voyage of *The Golden Hinde*.
● Give some reasons for Drake acting as he did.

Lesson organisation
Teacher-led discussion with the whole class; whole-class role-play followed by group work.

Vocabulary
The Golden Hinde
galleon
Pacific Ocean
compass

What you need and preparation

Find a picture of a sailing ship of Drake's time; you might be able to get pictures of the reconstruction of *The Golden Hinde*. You will also need: a globe and compass; photocopiable pages 108–10; scissors.

What to do

Introduction

Read the story on the photocopiable sheets to the children. Explain any unfamiliar vocabulary such as *galleon*, a large Spanish sailing ship. Tell the children that Drake's ship was originally called *The Pelican* – a *hind* is a female deer (*hinde* is the Elizabethan spelling).

Discuss the story in its geographical context, inviting one or two of the children to come out to the front of the class to help you find England and the Americas on the globe. Ensure that the children are aware that the blue indicates the sea, and understand that Drake had to find ways around the land masses. Emphasise that the world is like a ball and if you keep going in the same direction you end up where you started. Indicate the direction of Drake's voyage, and show where the Spanish ships were waiting off Brazil and Argentina. When you talk about sailing around Cape Horn into the Pacific, show how close the Antarctic is and emphasise the bad weather and danger. Drake then sailed up the West Coast of South America, raiding. He stopped off in California for water and repairs, before setting off across the Pacific, through the Indian Ocean, round the Cape of Good Hope and home. Show the children the compass and talk about how Drake used it to find his way.

CHAPTER 1
FAMOUS PEOPLE

Men of their time

Follow-up activity
Let the children use globes and maps to follow other well-known routes around the world.

Use the picture of *The Golden Hinde*, or a sailing ship of Drake's time, to talk about the differences between that type of ship and modern ships. Emphasise how small it was, that it moved by wind power, that they needed to stop for food and water.

(30 mins) Development

Now role-play a voyage on *The Golden Hinde* with the whole class. Ask the children to sit on the carpet and pretend that they are on the ship. Can they imagine themselves at sea? What would it have felt like? Emphasise in the role-play the rough seas, the cramped conditions, the scariness of not knowing where you are and where you are going. Give them ideas about what they would need to do, such as consulting the compass to tell the helmsman which way to steer.

After the role-play, ask the children why they think Drake decided to sail around the world. (To avoid the Spanish fleet; because he knew the world was round; to avoid going around Cape Horn again.) Split the children into groups, giving each group a copy of photocopiable page 110 and explain that they must cut out the statements and sort them into two categories: those that give Drake's point of view and those that give the sailor's.

(10 mins) Plenary

Conduct a brief class role-play in which Francis Drake and the sailor hold a debate to put forward their different points of view.

Differentiation

Encourage more able children to make a list of arguments 'for' and 'against' – the sailor's opinion that the world is flat versus Drake's opinion that the world is round, and so on – without using photocopiable page 110. They can consult the story on photocopiable pages 108 and 109. Less confident readers may need help to read and arrange the statements on photocopiable page 110.

Assessing learning outcomes

Can the children explain why Drake sailed around the world? Can they retell the story?

(1 hour) Who was Samuel Pepys?

Learning objectives
● Make interpretations of the past.
● Answer questions using certain sources.
● Place events in order.

Lesson organisation
Teacher-led discussion with the whole class; individual work.

Background information

The account of the Great Fire of London (see photocopiable pages 111 and 112) is intended as an introduction to work on the diaries of Pepys and Evelyn and it includes material from both. You can of course go straight to using extracts from these but they are quite difficult and the children will probably understand them better if they know the story already.

There are various websites about the London Fire Brigade; www.jmccall.demon.co.uk/brigade.htm is quite good. The Museum of London and the London Fire Brigade Museum have relevant displays.

What you need and preparation

Obtain the original accounts from Pepys diary (Sept 2nd 1666) and/or Evelyn's (for Sept 3rd, 4th and 5th); www.thehistorynet.com/BritishHeritage/articles/1995_text.htm has extracts. You will also need: pictures of Tudor houses, photocopiable pages 111 and 112; photocopiable page 113 (copies cut up for sequencing).

Men of their time

What to do

20 mins **Introduction**
Read the story on photocopiable pages 111 and 112 and talk about the things that happen in it. Key points for emphasis are:

● London was a medieval city built with timber-framed houses. (Show pictures of Tudor houses. Point out how close together they were and how the fire could spread. Discuss what burns easily and what does not. Talk about fire safety.)

● There was no fire brigade nor were there any fire engines.

● London was very small and you could bump into the king and lord mayor walking the streets. King Charles walked his dogs every day in St James's Park and politely greeted everyone he met.
   Use the discussion to help the children to answer the key questions:

● Why did the fire spread so easily?

● How was it put out?

20 mins **Development**
Give out a set of story sections cut out from photocopiable page 113 to each child and ask them to sequence the story of Samuel Pepys and the Great Fire of London.

20 mins **Plenary**
Call the class together to review the correct sequence of the pictures and captions on photocopiable page 113.

Differentiation

Use photocopiable page 113 with the pictures separated from the captions so that more able children have to put them together before sequencing both. Children who find it difficult to read the captions can fill in speech bubbles, with the help of an adult, to add to each section of the story, once the pictures have been pasted onto a large sheet of paper.

Assessing learning outcomes

Can the children sequence the story? Can they answer simple questions about Pepys and the fire after listening to the story? If you use original extracts from Pepys and Evelyn, can the children make some distinctions between the accounts?

Vocabulary
nightshirt
thatched
Tower of London
Lord Mayor
St Paul's Cathedral
secret code
account

Follow-up activities
● Good readers could use extracts from the original sources to answer questions.
● The story lends itself to role-play, perhaps for an assembly.
● Children could work on their own secret codes. Simple substitution of letters is easiest. One way of doing this is to have two small alphabet strips positioned so that they can be moved like a slide rule – when you want to write *a* you look above and write *c* instead, and so on.

(1 hour) Who was William Hogarth?

Background information

William Hogarth was born in Smithfield in 1697 and died in Chiswick in 1764. He was primarily an engraver but became a respected painter. His great legacy is in the wonderful prints that surge with London life. He did several series of prints that unfolded moral tales, like *The Rake's Progress* and *Marriage à la Mode*. This story is based around the 1741 print *The Enraged Musician*, which Key Stage 1 children should particularly enjoy.

What you need and preparation

Find a reproduction of *The Enraged Musician* and reproductions of other Hogarth prints. These can be found on www.lamp.ac.uk/hogarth – the University of Wales' Hogarth archive, which has most prints online. You will also need: photocopiable pages 114 and 115; Jenny Uglow's *Hogarth: a Life and a World* (Faber & Faber) – optional; paper and board or flip chart (or prepared worksheet – see 'Development'); writing materials.

Learning objective
Find answers from sources on the basis of simple observation or in ways that go beyond simple observation.

Lesson organisation
Teacher-led discussion with the whole class; group work.

**Men of their
time**

What to do

Introduction
30 mins Read the story on the photocopiable sheets to the children. Explain difficult vocabulary such as *thumbnail*, a small drawing, the size of a thumbnail (the fact that Hogarth literally made thumbnail sketches is reported by his friend John Nichol in his *Biographical Anecdotes of William Hogarth*); *burin*, a steel chisel used for engraving; *sedan chair*, a closed chair for one passenger carried on poles by two men, one in front and one behind (these were characteristic of the 18th century); *hautboy*, an instrument like an oboe.

Discuss the story, stressing the following key points:
● Hogarth told stories in his pictures.
● We can learn a lot about his time by looking at them.

Jenny Uglow's *Hogarth: a Life and a World* contains some reproductions of Hogarth's prints, which you could show to the children at this point, if you have a copy.

Now show the children a reproduction of *The Enraged Musician* and discuss what they can see in it. Ask questions such as:
● What is happening in the picture?
● What are the people doing?
● What sort of clothes did they wear in those days?
● What do you think the characters are saying?

Development
20 mins Split the children into groups and give out reproductions of Hogarth prints, one to each group. Write down some questions on the board for them to answer (or distribute the worksheets you have prepared based on the following questions):
● Write down all the noises that you could hear if you were standing in that street.
● Why do you think that the musician in the window is angry?
● Would you have liked to have lived in Hogarth's London?
● Why do you think that?

Plenary
10 mins Discuss the children's answers to the questions on Hogarth's paintings.

Differentiation
Less able children could talk about the picture they have been allocated rather than write. Let children who finish the questions quickly write a story about what is going on in the picture. If you prepare worksheets on Hogarth's paintings, they could be differentiated.

Assessing learning outcomes
Can the children find answers from the picture on the basis of simple observation or in ways that go beyond simple observation?

55 mins Who was Isambard Kingdom Brunel?

Background information

Brunel was born in Portsmouth in 1806. He was involved in a huge number of projects various in nature including the Thames tunnel, the Clifton suspension bridge, steamships like the Great Western and the Great Eastern and the Bristol Docks improvement. The GWR was probably his greatest achievement. He designed all the tunnels, embankments, bridges and viaducts along with stations and rolling stock. It is easy to find pictures of him – short and square with an enormous top hat and a big cigar. He characterises the Victorian age in his confidence that he could design and build absolutely anything. There are few places in Britain far from Victorian constructions in iron and steel, and so it should be relatively easy to see Brunel's own works. They were built to last!

What you need and preparation

Obtain a map showing the area between London and Bristol, or a map of the Victorian railway network. You will also need: photocopiable pages 116 and 117; photocopiable page 118 (copies cut up into individual statements).

What to do

20 mins Introduction
Read the story on photocopiable pages 116 and 117 to the children, then highlight the following key points through discussion:
- Building the railway was a huge undertaking involving bridges, tunnels, stations and embankments.
- The land had to be carefully measured and mapped before anything could be done.
- The engineers had to think of the best route for the trains over level firm ground.
- Brunel succeeded because of persistence, hard work and detailed planning.
- There were no JCBs or mechanical diggers. Everything was done with pick and shovel, horse and cart and dynamite!
- Not everyone thought it was a good idea.

25 mins Development
Split the class into two groups, asking one or two children in each group to be key speakers. Give out a set of arguments (from photocopiable page 118) 'for' and 'against' the building of a new railway in Brunel's time, giving a different set to each group. Each group must discuss the statements and also think of other points that they could put forward. Allow them about 15 minutes to discuss the arguments and then bring the class back together again. Invite the key speakers from each group to put their arguments to the whole class.

10 mins Plenary
After the debate, let the class vote for or against the railway. Stress that the children must make their votes based on their own individual opinions rather than simply taking the point of view that their side of the debate expressed.

Differentiation

Use adult support to help children structure their debate and to explain the statements that they have been given.

Assessing learning outcomes

Can the children understand and give reasons for different opinions about the railways?

Learning objective
Give reasons why people in the past acted as they did.

Lesson organisation
Teacher-led discussion with the whole class; group and individual work.

Vocabulary
britschka
drawing board
theodolite
parliament
tunnel
design and technology

Follow-up activities
- Ask the children to draw themselves as a Victorian character, using books to research costume. They can add a speech bubble giving their opinion on the railway and reasons for it.
- Hold discussions on what improves and harms the environment.

Men of their time

55 mins Who is Nelson Mandela?

Learning objective
Recognise why people did things and what happened as a result.

Lesson organisation
Teacher-led discussion with the whole class; group work.

Vocabulary
South Africa
Afrikaans
India
Gujarati
Punjabi
Xhosa Zulu
the Rainbow Nation

ICT opportunities
Ask the children to word-process their completed group response sheets.

Follow-up activity
Encourage the children to share their opinions on things that matter to them and explain their views. Help them to recognise what is fair and unfair and what is right and wrong.

Background information
Nelson Mandela retired from his position of President of the Republic of South Africa in 1999. He was born in 1918, so his life spans most of the 20th century; it represents history at its freshest. He is seen by many as the greatest hero of our time; by others as a terrorist. Like all historical figures, his life will be assessed and analysed again and again. It is dangerous to view any historical figure as superhuman or wholly good or bad, but the more recent they are the more it seems to matter! One of the beauties of history is that it can allow us to take partisan positions in a safer 'virtual world' of the past. When dealing with issues closer to home it is all the more important to take a balanced view and analyse what people did and why. A wise teacher will avoid portraying a superman whilst stressing the message of reconciliation.

What you need and preparation
Find some short biographies and pictures of Nelson Mandela in reference books – information can also be obtained through Internet search engines like www.ask.co.uk. There is a full biography at www.anc.org.za/people/mandela. His autobiography, *Long Walk to Freedom* is published by Abacus. You will also need: photocopiable page 119; prepared group response sheets – see 'Development'; writing materials.

What to do
25 mins Introduction
Read the story on photocopiable page 119 to the children. In a discussion, bring out the following key points:
● Conflicts are more likely to be resolved by a willingness to talk and respect one's opponents.
● South African society (and ours) is a mixture of cultures and races and this should be seen as a great strength.
● It is important to struggle for what you think is right, but it is also important how you do it.

20 mins Development
Split the children into groups and ask them to discuss the story and use additional reference materials to fill in a group response sheet. This should be structured as follows:
● We have found out three things about South Africa:
● We have found out three things about Nelson Mandela:
● We think Nelson Mandela is a great man because…

10 mins Plenary
Invite children to give feedback to the rest of the class about their findings on South Africa and Nelson Mandela. Encourage them to compare their conclusions on why Nelson Mandela is a great man.

Differentiation
When children are completing their group response sheets, let less able children listen to the story on tape to find the answers. An adult helper could advise them on the places where it would be appropriate to stop the tape. The children's answers could also be recorded.

Assessing learning outcomes
Can the children give reasons for their opinions about Mandela?

Thematic studies

Two main tasks lie before teachers of history in Key Stage 1. On the one hand they must teach children how to 'do' history, they must develop the skills and understanding outlined in the Programme of Study. On the other, they must begin to build a framework of knowledge.

History is a subject heavy in content – a lifetime of study will not be sufficient to know all the facts about even a short period of the past. We pick up historical facts all the time, in books and films, on visits to new places, in newspapers and on television. The important thing is that we 'file' the facts in our memories in the right places. We need to make a timeline in our heads to contain all the information.

We may hear the story of King Alfred and the cakes at an early age, and the teacher shows pictures in which the men have cloaks and strings criss-crossed around the bottom half of their legs. If she does her job and emphasises words like 'Anglo-Saxon', then ever after those sorts of pictures will come to mind as we hear those words. We are creating a sort of historical stage set on which increasingly complex scenes can be enacted.

If children are to remember, and retain enduring images, then we must select material that is meaningful to them. Generally this will mean that we talk about aspects of the past that can be directly compared with aspects of their own lives. The National Curriculum speaks of 'the way of life' and 'lifestyles' though it no longer gives particular examples. In our thematic studies we look at lifestyle in different ways.

The 'seaside' study is about comparing the modern child's experience of holidays directly with that of another child at the beginning of the 20th century; the interest is generated by the positive associations of holidays. There are many opportunities to link with literacy in this study.

'Breadmaking through the ages' ranges over a very long timeline indeed, emphasising continuity in the human experience as well as change and variation. Work with timelines will be an essential part of this study and cross-curricular links with science and numeracy could be strong.

We have chosen to construct fairly substantial themes rather than give one-off lessons in order to give the opportunity to develop skills and understanding in a structured way whilst presenting a number of interlocking aspects of each theme.

The seaside at the turn of the century

Enquiry questions	Learning objectives	Teaching activities	Learning outcomes	Literacy links	Cross-curricular links
What is a holiday?	● Make distinctions between aspects of their own lives and those of other people. ● Order events from the past and use specific vocabulary.	Discuss the children's holidays and those of their immediate family. Investigate the origins of holidays.	Children: ● recognise specific similarities and differences about holidays now and in the past ● use historical terms when ordering events on the timeline	Make a collection of words linked to the topic.	Numeracy: data handling; sequencing and ordering time. RE: festivals and how these are related to holidays. Art: look at the medieval Book of Days and create a modern equivalent.
What were holidays like long ago and who went on them?	● Demonstrate factual knowledge and understanding of aspects of the past beyond living memory. ● Use specific vocabulary related to the period.	Storytelling followed by group activities to further investigate different aspects of the story.	● use vocabulary and images to demonstrate their understanding of the historical period	Speech marks and their use – transfer parts of the story into eyewitness accounts.	Art: class collage of a seaside scene.
How would people have got to the seaside long ago?	● Demonstrate factual knowledge and understanding of main events and changes. ● Give reasons for and results of main events and changes.	Investigate and discuss Victorian railway travel. Role-play activity to follow up.	● children use their role-play to demonstrate understanding of some of the changes that rail travel brought to the period	Poetry writing – use structures from poetry to write own poems from initial jottings and words.	Numeracy: use of timetables to plan routes and journeys. Science: forces – look at how steam pressure works as a force. Art: investigate the work of William Frith.

Enquiry questions	Learning objectives	Teaching activities	Learning outcomes	Literacy links	Cross-curricular links
What did people do at the seaside long ago?	● Find information from sources that go beyond simple observations – make deductions. ● Select and combine information from a variety of sources.	Use a variety of primary sources to describe some of the attractions found at the seaside.	● make deductions on the basis of the evidence ● use a variety of different sources to support their deductions	Investigate factual writing, suggesting questions and answering them from text. Shared writing in a similar style.	Numeracy: use of timetables Geography: growth of the seaside. Art: seaside images including postcards.
How did people have fun at the seaside long ago?	● Demonstrate factual knowledge and understanding of the past beyond living memory. ● Find answers to questions using sources that go beyond simple observations – make deductions.	Carousel a variety of activities looking at the different types of entertainment available at the seaside, music hall, band, Punch and Judy and the park.	● justify their answers through their use of different sources ● identify various aspects of the past by using specific vocabulary	Use simple songs to identify and discuss patterns of rhythm, rhyme and other features of sound.	Numeracy: use squared paper to design a geometrical garden. Geography: investigate environmental theme of tourism. Music: music hall songs; percussion.
How did people remember their holidays?	● Identify some of the ways in which the past is represented. ● Select and combine information from sources.	Use artefacts and postcards to put objects into their historical context.	● suggest different ways in which people remember their holidays ● use a range of strategies to answer questions about artefacts.	Use an artefact as a stimulus for shared story writing. Letter writing format – children look at postcards and write one of their own.	

CHAPTER 2
THEMATIC STUDIES

The seaside at
the turn of the
century

1 hour What is a holiday?

Learning objectives
● Make distinctions between aspects of their own lives and those of other people.
● Order events from the past and use specific vocabulary.

Lesson organisation
Teacher-led, whole-class discussion; whole-class and individual development and plenary work.

Background information

Initially festivals were linked to the church year – the word 'holiday' is derived from the 'holy day' observances of the past. Our holidays still follow this pattern to a certain extent, for example Christmas, Easter and Whitsun. Other holidays and festivals link to the agricultural year, such as harvest and summer. Most of these festivals were of a relatively short duration as people could not be spared from their work for too long.

The family holiday for all sections of the community is a relatively modern phenomenon. In the past, only the rich moved from town to country at different seasons. It was only with Victorian and Edwardian times that the middle classes began to take periods of time off to relax as a family unit. The working class and poor were unable to take a holiday until paid holiday allowances were introduced. Until this happened the best most people could hope for was a day trip or outing.

What you need and preparation

Collect together some reference material on holidays now and in the past, such as *Rural Life* by John Seymour (Collins & Brown), *Holidays* by Gill Tanner and Tim Wood (A&C Black), *Our Holidays* in the *Starting History* series (Wayland), *People Having Fun* in the *People Through History* series (Wayland). Prepare a pictorial timeline showing the months of the year and seasons (include key words such as *beginning, ending, month* and *season*). You will also need: photocopiable page 120 plus a covering letter to parents, carers or older relatives explaining the forthcoming topic and asking for their help (send out these two items beforehand as completed sheets will be needed for the activity); photocopiable page 121; board or flip chart; large sheet of paper; writing materials.

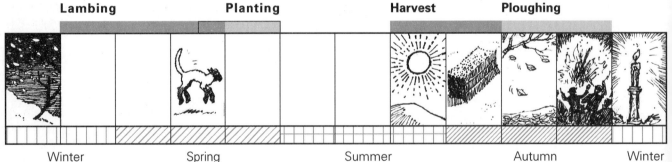

| Lambing | Planting | Harvest | Ploughing |

Winter   Spring   Summer   Autumn   Winter

What to do

20 mins Introduction

Hold an initial discussion to talk about the children's experiences of holidays and to establish a shared framework of vocabulary and understanding. Start with reference to the most recent holiday period (apart from summer), asking the children:

● What sort of thing did you do?
● Was this holiday different from the summer holidays; if so how was it different?
● What do we mean by 'holidays'? (Write a definition on the board and encourage the children to list different types of holidays and the time of year in which they have been taken.)

Move on to investigate the children's experiences of summer holidays:

● Who has been away on holiday over the summer?
● Where did you go?
● What did you do?
● What type of holiday was it?

Vocabulary
holiday
long ago
recently
nowadays
festival
outing
day trip
months
seasons
year

CHAPTER 2
THEMATIC STUDIES

The seaside at
the turn of the
century

Allow children to discuss answers to these questions in pairs or small groups and then share information with the rest of the class.

Collate the answers on a sheet of paper as a table, for example:

Place	Sort	Type
UK/abroad	hotel/caravan/camping/ staying with relatives	seaside/countryside/ sightseeing

Ask the children why they think we have holidays and encourage them to suggest possible reasons, for example to visit relatives, to relax, to attend a festival or to visit a particular place as a tourist. Show the children pictures from the reference material you have selected.

35 mins Development

Look at the completed questionnaries (photocopiable page 120) that have been returned from home. Invite the children to share the written responses and ask them the following questions:
- What does this information tell us about holidays in the past?
- What was the same and what was different?
- Did people go to the same places?
- Did they go for the same reasons?

Point out key facts which might include less travel abroad, less distance travelled, a different mode of travel (perhaps less air travel), and either more or less time spent on holiday.

Collate the answers on a sheet of paper, using the same format as before, and compare the two tables to pick out similarities and differences.

Take the timeline of the year and point out specific features and vocabulary, for example *beginning, ending, month, season*. Add information about the agricultural year and what comes when, such as lambing and planting (from February to April), harvesting (September and October), ploughing (October and November).

Use questions to provide a focus, for example:
- When does the year start and finish?
- Where do the seasons come?
- What are the different parts of the agricultural year? (Urban children will need plenty of input here.)

Once initial information has been added to the timeline, move on to discuss specific holidays or festivals. These could also be added to the timeline. Start with the main Christian festivals such as Christmas, Easter, Whitsun and May Day. Encourage the children to ask you to add other festivals they know about, for example Divali, Hallowe'en, Guy Fawkes Night, Purim, Chinese New Year, Eid.

Finally, ask:
- When do we get holidays? (Can the children see any correlation between the timeline and their time off school?)
- How do these dates relate to holidays in the past?
- How do these dates relate to the farming year?

Now provide the children with copies of photocopiable page 121 for them to complete.

5 mins Plenary

Invite the children to discuss their findings – that is, their answers to the first two questions on photocopiable page 121, and to share the conclusions they have drawn in answer to the third question.

ICT opportunities
● Enter information on children's holidays into a database or spreadsheet, and use data to draw charts.
● The children could word-process questionnaires for other children to answer.

Follow-up activity
Ask the children to draw illustrations for the class timeline, using textbooks, CD-ROMs and the Internet for reference.

CHAPTER 2
THEMATIC STUDIES

The seaside at
the turn of the
century

Differentiation

Give vocabulary sheets to less able children to help them fill in photocopiable page 121. They may also need the support of an adult helper. More able children could work together to complete two tables, one which gives data about holidays in the past ('Then'), the other about holidays today ('Now').

Assessing learning outcomes

Can the children recognise two or three similarities about holidays now and in the past? Can they recognise two or three differences about holidays now and in the past? Can they use historical terms when ordering events on the timeline?

(1 hour) What were holidays like long ago and who went on them?

Learning objectives
● Demonstrate factual knowledge and understanding of aspects of the past beyond living memory.
● Use specific vocabulary related to the period.

Lesson organisation
Teacher-led, whole-class storytelling session; group development work; whole-class plenary.

Vocabulary
growler
parasol
carpet bag
smelling salts
liver pills
smoke and steam
first, second, and third class
mint humbugs
promenade/prom
bathing suits
pier

What you need and preparation

Collect together some books which have images of Victorian and Edwardian scenes, for example *The British Century* by Brian Moynahan (Seven Dials) and *Faces of Britain* by N Hindmarch Keen (Blitz Editions, Amazon Publishing). A large poster of a Victorian/Edwardian seaside or street scene would be useful. You will also need: photocopiable pages 122–4 (preferably copied onto acetate for use with an overhead projector) and images that could be of Rosie's family from the story – large cut-out figures (essential for one of the group activities), photographs or puppets; paper; writing and drawing materials.

What to do

(30 mins) Introduction

Introduce the children to the period by looking at the textbooks and images of Victorian and Edwardian scenes. Ask:

● Does this look very different from your own time?
● Do you think that children went to the seaside then as we do now?

Tell the children that you are going to read them a story about Rosie's day. Explain that while this is not a true story it is based on the sorts of things that would have happened on a day trip to the seaside at this time. Read 'Rosie's day at the seaside', and explain specific words and terms, for example *growler* (a four-wheeled horse-drawn taxi), *parasol, carpet bag* (a soft holdall made of old Turkish carpet), *liver pills* (used for indigestion), *smoke and steam* (smoke came from the coal fire under the engine's boiler – this made steam to push the pistons in and out; the smoke came out of the chimney and the steam from the cylinders near the wheels), *first, second, and third class* (doors were labelled 1, 2 or 3 as trains had carriages to fit in with very clear social divisions).

(20 mins) Development

Split the children into groups to work on different activities in which they:

● play 'Historical I spy', using the textbooks or a large poster of a Victorian/Edwardian seaside or street scene to develop their understanding of historical vocabulary (they should try to use some of the specific terms from the story)
● use storyboards to sequence episodes from the story, using one from the beginning, one from the middle and one from the end
● research and then draw pictures of the different family members, ensuring that the detail of the costume is accurate
● draw speech bubbles on figures from the story, then write text in each speech bubble which is a comment on what the character liked best about the day.

CHAPTER 2
THEMATIC STUDIES

The seaside at
the turn of the
century

10 mins **Plenary**
Talk about what the children like about the seaside today. Are they the same sort of things as Rosie and her family enjoyed?

Differentiation
Enlist adult support to help with the use of vocabulary in the 'Historical I spy' game. Provide less able children with drawing activities rather than writing ones in the group work.

Assessing learning outcomes
Can the children demonstrate some of the features of a seaside holiday at the turn of the century through their use of images and vocabulary?

50 mins How would people have got to the seaside long ago?

Background information
The growth of the railways had a massive impact on life in the Victorian period. People, goods and information were now able to move quickly from one place to another. Before the advent of the railways, travel was very much affected by the weather and dependent on the speed of the horses. The railways opened up the countryside and brought people and ideas into the more isolated areas. It also allowed those from the country to travel with much greater ease into the large metropolitan areas.

What you need and preparation
Obtain a copy of William Frith's painting *The Railway Station* (either several small copies or one large poster-sized version, published by Kingfisher Publications). Find other images of railway travel. If possible, watch a video of episode 6 of *History of Art* (Channel 4) – this gives details about the picture, artist and how the artist selected the different elements; find video clips of steam trains in motion (for example, a scene from *The Railway Children*). Try to find copies of Victorian timetables and adverts for railway outings in your local history library. You will also need a board or flip chart.

What to do
15 mins **Introduction**
Divide the children into groups of three to five, and either nominate, or ask the children to select, a spokesperson for each group. Display the painting *The Railway Station*, or distribute small copies to groups, and ask the children to look at and discuss the picture for ten minutes. Then ask each spokesperson to give their group's response to the following questions:
● Where is this place?
● What do you think is happening?
● What impression does the picture give you? What does it make you think of? Think of four words that would describe this feeling.
● What makes you think that travelling by train is popular?

Learning objectives
● Demonstrate factual knowledge and understanding of main events and changes of a particular period.
● Give reasons for and results of main events and changes.

Lesson organisation
Group, then whole-class discussion; pairs activities.

The seaside at the turn of the century

Vocabulary
railway engine
steam train
terminus
station porter
travel
guard
station master
main/branch line
ticket collector
ticket booth
engine driver
fireman

ICT opportunities
● Use a CD-ROM containing appropriate photographs to search for reference material on steam trains in the Victorian and Edwardian period.
● Use the Internet to find information on modern day steam trains, for example the Bluebell Railway.

Follow-up activities
● Find out information on any local steam train attractions and arrange a visit. Or invite a steam railway enthusiast to come to the school to talk to the children.
● Visit a science museum and look at the development of steam power.
● Visit a local railway, take photographs of the station and talk to the staff about who uses the station now.
● Show a clip from a film such as *The Railway Children* to show the sights and sounds of a steam train in motion.

● Describe one person in detail and say where you think they are going.

Collate the responses from the groups, writing brief details on the board. Look at which characters have been chosen and the type of words used to describe the picture. Help the children to pick out other points:
● What does this tell you about who was travelling by rail?
● Where did the luggage go?
● Why do you think people were travelling? Can you tell from the picture? (Point out clues such as the cricket bat in the boy's hand.)

Introduce other images of railway travel in this period through photographs and paintings. What can the children deduce about the importance of the railways?

(20 mins) Development

Give the children some background information about how people travelled before the railways. Explain that travel was:
● slow – by horse/coach/post; horses needed to be changed on long journeys or take it in easy stages over several days or weeks
● dangerous – isolated roads led to the rise of highwaymen; accidents were more likely on dirt roads; people only travelled during daylight if possible
● difficult/uncomfortable – no tarmac on the roads, only dirt roads (or cobbled streets in town); bumpy ride in coaches; open to the elements so travel was difficult in bad weather.

Contrast the earlier type of transport with the railways, which were fast, efficient, regular, affordable.

Now encourage the children to compare present day train travel with train travel in the past. Help them to understand how their experiences of train travel will be very different from those in the past. Point out the differences:
● Steam, not diesel or electricity – this meant that you needed fuel (coal) and water, and a fireman, or stoker, to keep the fire going; engines were different (refer to the *Thomas the Tank Engine* stories, which most children will know).
● More people were needed to work the train – stokers, guards and ticket collectors in addition to the driver, and porters to carry bags.
● Different fares and carriages – first, second and third class (look at contemporary timetables if possible and price information).
Ask the children:
● Which would be the quickest journey?
● Which would be the cheapest?
● What would be the difference between first and third class?

(15 mins) Plenary

Ask the children to role-play in pairs two people who are travelling by steam train. Who are their characters (for example, shop girls on a day out, newlyweds, a cook and a nursery maid, a governess and a young child)? Where are they going to? In which class will they be travelling? How much will it cost? How are they feeling about the trip?

Differentiation
By outcome.

Assessing learning outcomes
Can the children give valid reasons for travelling by train? Can they demonstrate some of the changes that rail travel brought to the times?

CHAPTER 2
THEMATIC STUDIES

The seaside at
the turn of the
century

⓵hour What did people do at the seaside long ago?

Background information

The seaside first became popular around the beginning of the 19th century when salt water was recommended as a cure for all sorts of medical problems. Bathers did not usually swim in the sea, however. Sea water was brought to the hotels and the patient bathed in the comfort of their own room. The Prince Regent popularised Brighton, and later his younger sister convalesced for a couple of weeks down the coast at Worthing, making it a more respectable alternative to 'rakish' Brighton. Only the very rich could afford such holidays but, as the railway network spread, the cost of the fares came down and so the seaside holiday came within the means of the middle classes. By Edwardian times most of the population could afford at least an occasional day trip.

When swimming in the sea became popular, elaborate measures were considered necessary to preserve decency. Bathing machines were wooden changing huts on wheels. You could hire a bathing costume with the hut, and when you had changed, the hut was backed into the sea.

What you need and preparation

Gather together some photographs of Edwardian or Victorian seaside scenes (preferably of the same resort). You will also need: an enlarged copy of photocopiable pages 125 and 126; reference books; board or flip chart; paper; writing and drawing materials; railway posters advertising outings to a resort (optional).

What to do

⓴mins Introduction

Show the children the enlarged copy of photocopiable page 125, and establish that it is advertising a seaside resort called Worthing. Discuss the children's own experiences of visiting travel agents or looking at holiday brochures with their parents and carers.

Read through the text and point out specific vocabulary, *dressing tents, paddle steamers* and so on. Ask the children questions such as:

● What impression do you have of the place and why do you think that?
● What sort of entertainment does this place offer?
● How does this compare with what you do today at the seaside?
Show the children the photographs of the seaside resort and focus on the content by asking:
● What can you see in the photos?
● What type of place is it and how do you know this?
● What are the people doing?

Point out specific features that they might have missed, for example bathing machines, the type of clothing being worn, a bandstand and the promenade. Now ask the children if they can see any of the things mentioned in the first source. Write these down on the board, together with any questions that they might have.

㉚mins Development

Split the children into groups to work on tasks differentiated by ability (see 'Differentiation') in which they:

● design a poster to show different attractions at a seaside resort, using reference books and photographs – each person in the group must be responsible for at least one element of the poster
● choose a photograph, draw a picture of the scene depicted, copying the details, and write about four things they have noticed in it – they should then complete the statement *I think a visit to the seaside in Edwardian times was/was not fun because…*

CHAPTER 2
THEMATIC STUDIES

The seaside at
the turn of the
century

ICT opportunities
● Use an art program to design the poster, selecting a layout and including clip art borders.
● Word-process the written responses that accompany the drawing of the photograph.
● Word-process the journal, letter or descriptive account, selecting fonts and layout.

Follow-up activities
● Visit a travel agent to find out about holidays in the same resort today – the accommodation, the attractions that are on offer, and so on.
● Research the more recent past through oral history, asking children to interview their grandparents or great-grandparents. You could also use television or video footage, for example *How We Used to Live* (Channel 4/Leisure).

● take part in shared writing with adult support, writing a journal entry, a letter or a simple descriptive account entitled 'The first time at the seaside', each child contributing ideas – illustrations could be added later
● complete photocopiable page 126.

10 mins **Plenary**

Nominate a spokesperson for each group and ask them to explain what their group's task has been. Invite individual children to show their finished work to the rest of the class. Have any of the questions raised in the introduction been answered? Is there anything that the children still want to find out?

Differentiation

Help children who are creating the poster to structure their work and allocate tasks.

Less able children may need more advice about layout. Encourage more able children to carry out research for the poster content.

For the group who are copying the photograph, help children with lower-ability language skills by providing them with a vocabulary sheet or a writing frame for the written element.

Language ability is less important for the shared writing task, as adult support will be provided, but allow more able children to offer ideas too.

The task on photocopiable page 126 is suitable for lower-ability groups.

Assessing learning outcomes

Can the children make deductions on the basis of the evidence? Can they use a variety of different sources to support their deductions?

1 hour 15 mins # How did people have fun at the seaside long ago?

Learning objectives
● Demonstrate factual knowledge and understanding of the past beyond living memory.
● Find answers to questions using sources that go beyond simple observations – make deductions.

Lesson organisation
Whole-class explanation of activities; group development; plenary.

Background information

The seaside at the turn of the century offered a wide range of entertainment for all ages. Music halls and theatres were very popular and generally provided a variety of entertainment, with plenty of opportunity for audience participation. Magic and illusion acts were very popular along with acrobatic or juggling artists. The bandstand was often manned by military bands, with much of the repertoire being marches or popular tunes from the music halls. Punch and Judy men travelled up and down the country, entertaining children very much as they do now.

Parks were a source of civic pride and most were beautifully maintained. They were places to be seen 'promenading' in, and many offered a wide range of facilities. Most had some form of water feature. The long pier, which usually also had many amusement facilities, was another popular attraction.

What you need and preparation

Try to obtain some or all of the following: pictures of music halls and theatres, playbills, images of theatre artistes, a tape of music hall songs; a video extract showing a music hall performance. You will also need: dressing-up clothes (long dresses, bags, boas, top hats, boaters and so on); chairs arranged around a table and patio umbrella (as a pretend bandstand); a sign with details of the concert; prepared programme sheets; Punch and Judy puppets or some other hand puppets; reference books; period photographs of people in parks; photocopiable pages 127 and 128; paper, writing and drawing materials.

CHAPTER 2
THEMATIC STUDIES

The seaside at
the turn of the
century

What to do

Introduction

5 mins Explain to the children that the aim of the session is to allow them to consider what it would have been like to spend a day at the seaside at the turn of the 20th century. To help them to do this they will each work on a number of activities, completing a section of the photocopiable sheet before moving on.

Development

1 hour Split the children into groups to work on activities in which they:

● look at images of theatre and music halls, and if possible watch a video clip from a music hall performance such *The Good Old Days*. This should be followed by the children drawing a picture of a music hall scene, using reference books to ensure accuracy (the first question on photocopiable page 128).

● look at the sources of information (photographs of people in parks) and role-play an afternoon in the park, arranging the chairs for a concert around the 'bandstand'. The children can put on hats, boas and other dressing-up clothes, pick up a programme and listen to the tape of the music, before answering the second question on photocopiable page 128.

● take part in puppet theatre by using glove puppets for play, followed by research on 'Punch and Judy' on a CD-ROM or though the Internet. Information they have found should be printed out and attached to photocopiable page 128.

● look at the sources of information (photographs of people in parks), study the map of the park on photocopiable page 127 and complete the third and fourth questions on photocopiable page 128.

Plenary

10 mins Encourage children from each group to talk about the activities they have been doing to the rest of the class.

Differentiation

By outcome. Provide less able children with a vocabulary sheet to help them complete the written elements of photocopiable page 128. Alternatively, they could dictate their answers to an adult helper.

Assessing learning outcomes

Have the children justified their answers through their use of the different sources? Have they identified various aspects of the past by using specific vocabulary?

Vocabulary
music hall
artiste
entertainer
variety
theatre
performance
bandstand
orchestra
promenade
puppets
pier
sightseers
avenue
boating lake
rustic
refreshment

ICT opportunities
Develop reference skills through the use of CD-ROMs and the Internet.

Follow-up activities
● Have a singalong of some music hall favourites such as 'Daisy, Daisy' and 'Roll out the Barrel'.
● Let the children design a playbill using a graphics program, such as *Fine Artist*.

How did people remember their holidays?

1 hour 5 mins

Background information

Once people began to make day trips and take summer holidays they also began to want to have some way of remembering them. Mass production allowed souvenirs, such as china trinkets, to be produced cheaply. A large market grew up as people bought them for themselves or their friends. The picture postcard became increasingly popular as photography and production techniques improved.

In this activity, the children are asked to produce a piece of writing which describes an artefact, and you may find the book *Learning from Objects: a Teacher's Guide* by G Durbin *et al* (English Heritage) useful for reference.

Learning objectives
● Identify some of the different ways in which the past is represented.
● Select and combine information from sources.

Lesson organisation
Whole-class discussion; group activity; plenary.

CHAPTER 2
THEMATIC STUDIES

The seaside at
the turn of the
century

Vocabulary
momento
remember
souvenir
memory
postcard
trinket

**ICT
opportunities**
Use a program to
create a branching
system to
categorise and sort
the artefacts
investigated in the
activity.

What you need and preparation

Collect together some examples of holiday souvenirs, such as china trinkets which have pictures of different holiday locations on them; if possible look for some older examples – try junk shops and boot fairs. Obtain a range of postcards – humorous ones as well as those showing pictures of landscapes, attractions, monuments and so on. Try to get some original postcards from the turn of the century. These will also have the messages and the postage on the back which will add to the children's interest. You will also need: modern souvenirs and postcards (invite children to bring in some of theirs); board or flip chart; writing materials. Set up some tables in the centre of the room so that the children will all be involved and handle the artefacts safely.

What to do

(40 mins) Introduction

Select one of the souvenirs to use as an example, and pass it around the class. Allow the children to look closely at the artefact and encourage them to ask questions, for example what is it made of, who might have used it? (Write the question words on the board, such as *who, what, when* to help them.) Add questions yourself, if necessary, so that they fall into these main areas:
- technology – what is it made of and how is it made?
- condition – are there signs of wear? What about original colour?
- style – does it fit a period and does this agree with the technology?
- inscriptions – are there any written clues?
- function – practical and social; who might have used it? (Keep this to the end if possible.)

Once you have a good supply of questions – you should be able to generate about ten – begin to answer them. Encourage the children to come up with suggestions, but explain that not all of the questions can be answered immediately. Some can be answered on the basis of observations (for example, *What is it made of?*). Some will need to be researched using reference books, the Internet or experts such as local museum staff, for example *When was it made?* Some may not be able to be answered at all, for example *Who bought this?*

(20 mins) Development

Split the class into groups, give an artefact to each group and ask the children to examine it themselves using the same technique of investigation. Enlist adult helpers to be on hand to help them carry out research, using books and the Internet, to put the artefact into its historical context. Explain that they are welcome to make deductions to explain areas that cannot be answered on the basis of observation or fact.

The children can then record their investigations through a close observational drawing and a piece of factual writing which describes the object.

(5 mins) Plenary

Select one or two pieces of the children's work to show to the rest of the class and allow the children to describe what they have found out and what they think about the objects. Through discussion answer the question, *How do people remember their holidays?* Show the children modern day equivalents of some of the souvenirs, as a comparison.

Differentiation

By outcome. Expect more able children to justify their statements, for example *I think this because…*

Assessing learning outcomes

Can the children suggest different ways in which people remember their holidays? Can they use a range of strategies to answer questions about their artefacts?

**Follow-up
activity**
Visit a local
museum to look at
the work that a
museum does in
conserving,
cataloguing and
storing its
artefacts.

Breadmaking through the ages

Enquiry questions	Learning objectives	Teaching activities	Learning outcomes	Literacy links	Cross-curricular links
What do we know about bread?	• Communicate their findings in a variety of ways.	Look at a variety of bread from different cultures and countries, including white/ brown, leavened/ unleavened. Children share their experiences and ideas about the place of bread in everyday life.	Children: • select and describe a type of bread • explain and justify their choice. Class response: • Multimedia collage of bread display	Text work (Year 1) – assemble information from their own experiences, to write simple non-chronological reports. Write labels for drawings and produce extended captions.	Numeracy: data-handling – solve a given problem by sorting, classifying and organising data; discuss and explain results; classify and sort bread in a variety of ways;
How long have people been eating bread?	• Use terms concerned with the passing of time. • Order events and objects chronologically.	Exposition to look at pictures of bread and breadmaking from a variety of different periods. Discuss differences. Timeline images.	• use terms associated with time • order information chronologically	Vocabulary extension – make collections of new words linked to particular topics (Create class dictionary of bread and breadmaking.)	Numeracy: understand and use the vocabulary related to time; order events in time.
How was wheat milled in the past?	• Demonstrate factual knowledge and understanding of aspects of the past beyond living memory. • Give reasons why people in the past acted as they did.	Read 'The Little Red Hen'. Problem solving session – wheat needs to be crushed before it can be used. How this might be done. Look at hand milling/windmills/ watermills. Arrange a visit if possible.	• explain how wheat was milled in the past • explain why milling in the past was effective	Retell stories, giving main points in sequence. Discuss reasons for or causes of incidents in stories. Represent outlines of story plots using a variety of methods to record main events in order. Base the session on 'The Little Red Hen'.	Design and technology: look at how the different systems for milling are powered and at specific mechanisms, eg cogs and gears. Numeracy: know seasons of the year, eg sequence the life cycle of wheat. Science: living processes – life cycle of wheat.

Enquiry questions	Learning objectives	Teaching activities	Learning outcomes	Literacy links	Cross-curricular links
What was it like to be a baker in the past?	●Find answers from sources that go beyond simple observations – make deductions.	Look at pictures and documentary accounts of bakers at work.	●complete the statements about bakers in the past ●list and describe three other things found out about breadmaking or bakers.		Science: look at the process of breadmaking and how it works, eg effect of yeast on dough (Physical processes). Science/design and technology: look at ovens in the past and how they worked. Build oven in the grounds.
How has breadmaking changed?	●Make distinctions between aspects of their own lives and those of past times.	Visit to bakery in local supermarket or local bakery to gain firsthand experience of modern breadmaking.	●identify at least three differences between breadmaking in the past and in the present, and give explanations for the changes.	Write simple account of visit; use captions, pictures and arrows to record the main events in order to make a class book or wall story.	Numeracy: measures – investigate weight in relation to ingredients for recipes.

1 hour How long have people been eating bread?

Background information

Bread has been a staple part of the human diet from some of the earliest times. It is possible that the desire to cultivate cereals led to the change of lifestyle from hunter-gatherer societies to that of the first farmers. Archaeological remains have been found in human settlements that flourished 8000 years ago. Bread has proved to be a staple foodstuff because of its versatility and relative cheapness, and the basic process has changed little over the years. Children will have many experiences of different types of bread, reflecting different cultures and countries of origin. Stone Age civilisations made solid cakes from stone-crushed barley and wheat. Bread was an important element of the Egyptian diet, as can be seen from the evidence in paintings, hieroglyphs and mummified remains of loaves. The Egyptians were also probably the first people to produce leavened bread using yeast. Both the ancient Greeks and the ancient Romans liked their bread white, although this was generally out of the reach of ordinary people. The bakehouse was an important element of the household from the medieval period to the Victorians. The word 'pantry' comes from the medieval castle's bread store or 'painetterie'. Flat loaves, known as 'trenchers', served as plates in all but the richest households and were either eaten at the end of the meal or given to the poor. White bread or 'manchet' was always the food of the rich, while the poor relied on coarse black or brown bread. This was made from a variety of poorer quality cereals and often included peas or beans when times were hard. It is not until relatively modern times and cheap cultivation and manufacturing methods that white wheaten loaves have been available to all.

More information can be found in the following books: *Food in Antiquity* by D and P Brothwell (Johns Hoskins University Press), *Behind the Scenes* by Christina Hardyment (National Trust), *Our Daily Bread* by R Tames (Penguin), *Food in History* by R Tannahill (Penguin). Children's reference books include *Investigating Food in History* by Lisa Chaney (National Trust) and *Food in History* by S Robertson (Wayland).

What you need and preparation

Select children's reference books detailing domestic life from various periods and including images of breadmaking or people eating in the past. Prepare a large timeline with different periods marked on it (you may want to follow the periods detailed for Key Stage 2 plus the medieval period) and, if possible, cut out some images of breadmaking to represent different periods. You will also need: photocopiable pages 129 and 130 (for 'Differentiation'); board or flip chart; writing materials.

What to do

20 mins Introduction

Begin by finding out what the children already know about bread. Continue the discussion by asking:

● How long have people been eating bread?
● How do we know this?

Collate the children's answers on the board. Then show them the timeline with the different periods marked on it. Do they think people ate bread in Ancient Egypt, for example? Give them a brief history of the development of bread over the centuries. Refer to the images in the reference books which illustrate the different periods, and pick out an image of breadmaking, or of people eating in the past, for each period of the timeline (if you have any images that you have previously cut out, fix them to the timeline). Try to develop the children's understanding of the past by linking the topic of bread to other history work, perhaps relating it to famous people and famous events that the children may have studied.

Learning objectives
● Use terms concerned with the passing of time.
● Order events and objects chronologically.

Lesson organisation
Teacher-led discussion; group activities; whole-class plenary.

Vocabulary
ancient
period
long ago
Romans
Greeks
Egyptians
medieval
Tudor
Victorian
modern
now
evidence
hieroglyph
account

ICT opportunities
● Word-process the results of research carried out to complete photocopiable page 129 and use a graphics program to present work, inserting frames and clip art.
● Develop research skills using the Internet to find out further information.

Follow-up activities
● Read *Master Bun the Baker's Boy* by Allan Ahlberg (Puffin Books) to the children.
● Turn the home corner into a baker's shop, and show the children a nursery rhyme book that includes 'Hot Cross Buns', such as Nicola Bayley's *Book of Nursery Rhymes* (Cape).

30 mins ### Development
Split the children into groups to look at the different periods in the history of breadmaking, and allocate a different period to each group. Give out copies of the research writing frame on photocopiable page 129 for their group investigation, together with appropriate reference books. Allow the children to research their own period, in order to complete the photocopiable sheet, and tell them that you will be inviting them to offer you further information that could be added to the timeline.

10 mins ### Plenary
Take different elements from each group's completed work to add to the timeline.

Differentiation
Provide less able children with copies of photocopiable page 130 and ask them to cut out the mixed-up sections and group them correctly and in order of time.

Assessing learning outcomes
Can the children use terms associated with time when presenting their group responses? Can the children who worked on photocopiable page 130 order the different information chronologically?

---

1 hour # How was wheat milled in the past?

Learning objectives
● Demonstrate factual knowledge and understanding of aspects of the past beyond living memory.
● Give reasons why people in the past acted as they did.

Lesson organisation
Teacher-led introduction; practical problem solving in groups; whole-class plenary.

Background information
The most nutritious part of the grain is the kernel, and it was necessary to find ways to separate the edible from the inedible portion of the grain. Originally this process would have taken place at home, using simple millstones to grind the grain and produce a rough type of flour. As settlements grew and people discovered how to harness the power of wind and water, larger commercial premises were built. The miller became a person of some status within a community. Many millers became quite wealthy, often because they were not as scrupulously honest as they could have been. As the miller was able to keep a proportion of what he milled as payment, many took more than their fair share – hence the expression 'the miller's golden thumb' as he held the weights down to give the impression that the customer had more flour than he or she actually received! Evidence for windmills dates back to the 12th century, and they were probably preceded by watermills and animal power. Information on where to find mills (both watermills and windmills) can be found on the Internet, as can plenty of specific information about how they work. The following websites are most useful: www.botham.co.uk/bread/mill1.htm; www.botham.co.uk/bread/grain.htm; www.merton-online.co.uk/mo/plaza/leisure/places/windmill.asp (Wimbledon Windmill Museum); www. spab.org.uk (Society for the Protection of Ancient Buildings, Mills Section); www.spoom.org.uk (Society for the Preservation of Old Mills); www.geocities,com/Yosemite/1001/windhist.htm (history of windmills).

What you need and preparation
Collect together examples of different types of cereal, different types of flour and different types of bread (for example, sunflower, pumpernickel, multigrain, sun-dried tomato). You will also need: a copy of the story of the Little Red Hen; large stones, or pestle and mortar, and wheat or maize grains for grinding; a diagram of a cross-section of wheat; pictures of working mills; a model windmill; a video clip of a working mill (optional); paper; writing materials.

What to do

20 mins Introduction

Read the story of the Little Red Hen, then talk to the children about the breadmaking process – that it was laborious; help was needed; it was not something that could be done at home. Ask the children questions such as:

- Why didn't people mill their own wheat?
- What would they need to do to be able to grind their own grain?
- What types of grain could you use to make bread?

30 mins Development

Explain to the children that the aim of the session is to help them to understand why grain has to be milled and how this was done in the past. The challenge will be for them to find out the information themselves from a variety of practical activities, with each child taking part in each activity. These are tasks in which they:

- take some wheat grains and try to grind them between two stones or with a pestle and mortar. The adult supporting the group should ask the children questions such as:
  - What do you think would be needed in order for this to work?
  - Why were stones corrugated?
  - What types of stone could have been used? (Hard stone such as granite.)

This should be followed by the children looking at pictures of working mills, before they give responses (either as a group or by writing individually) to complete the following statements:
  - It was hard/easy to…
  - I liked/didn't like…
  - When you grind wheat…

- investigate the different types of cereal, looking carefully at the differences in the grain. You can give support to this group yourself, asking the children why they think the grain should be milled. Could it not be used just as it is? Help the children to try to decide which would make the best flour by looking at the seed. Look at different types of flour and different types of bread (sunflower, pumpernickel, multigrain, sun-dried tomato and so on). Show a diagram of a cross-section of wheat. Discuss the parts of the grain. How would you separate the different parts and just get the bit you needed? Talk about why wheat had to be threshed. Demonstrate if possible. Discuss how different parts of the grain are used for different types of bread. Talk about the need to mill and then sieve the flour. What is used for white bread? What is used for wholegrain? What does *granary* mean? In the past people were so keen to eat white bread that bakers used to add lime or alum to it to make it look whiter even though it made it taste horrid. Ask the children which type of bread is most nutritious.

- look at pictures of watermills and windmills, then answer the following questions individually:
  - What do you think makes this mill work?
  - Why do you think that this mill has been built here?
  - Can you think of any reason why the mill might not be working?
  - Do you think it is quicker to grind your corn yourself or to get the mill to do it for you? Why do you think this?

10 mins Plenary

Explain how a mill worked in the past. Demonstrate though the use of a model how the wheel or sails were able to turn the mill wheels. Show a video clip of a working mill, if possible.

Refer to the present and how mills have changed. What is the main change? Most mills are now powered by electricity and use horizontal rollers. Talk about experiences the children may have had if they have visited old mills – what did they notice the most?

Vocabulary

miller
mill
watermill
windmill
millstones
corrugated
sieve
mesh
cogs
gears
shaft
thresh
harvest
grind
cereal
wheat
barley
rye
oats
wholegrain
wheatgerm
granary

ICT opportunities
Use Internet facilities and CD-ROMs to research windmills and watermills and to find the nearest working mill.

**Follow-up
activity**
Arrange a visit to a
working mill, or to
a museum that has
an exhibit which
includes a
demonstration of
how a mill worked.

Differentiation

Let an adult act as a scribe for the first group activity to enable less able children to complete the statements. Provide an illustrated vocabulary sheet for children who need help in answering the questions in the third activity.

Assessing learning outcomes

Can the children explain how wheat was milled in the past? Can they explain why milling in the past was effective?

① What was it like to be a baker in the past?
hour

**Learning
objective**
Find answers from
sources that go
beyond simple
observations –
make deductions.

**Lesson
organisation**
Teacher-led
discussion;
individual activity;
whole-class
plenary.

Vocabulary
baker
oven
paddle
peel
shovel
knead
dough
ferment
yeast
mould

Background information

Machines in the bakehouse are a relatively modern phenomenon. For centuries bread was baked in a traditional manner. After the bread had been kneaded and proved it was baked in a brick oven. This was heated by faggots of wood, the ashes being scraped out when the oven was hot enough for baking. Bread was baked first, then cakes, pies and tarts. Bakehouses were often situated near or next to breweries, as yeast was an important part of the process. Big houses had bakehouses or baking ovens and so baked their own bread until the end of the Victorian period. Within the town, commercial bakers supplied bread; in country areas, families continued to bake their own bread. Baking was an important skill, as bread remained a staple part of most people's diets.

What you need and preparation

Find some images of traditional bakers (children will enjoy looking at *Master Bun The Baker's Boy* by Allan Ahlberg, Puffin Books, for example) and images and descriptions of traditional bakeries or bakehouses (see *Behind the Scenes* by Christina Hardyment, National Trust). You will also need: a recipe for bread, for example from *Mrs Beeton's Book of Household Management* (Chancellor Press) – optional; photocopiable pages 131 and 132; board or flip chart; writing materials.

What to do

30 **Introduction**
mins Show the children an image of a bakery or bakehouse, for example from *Behind the Scenes* by Christina Hardyment. Ask them:
● What do you think is happening in this room?
● How do you know that?
Point out significant facts and features and ask the children questions such as:
● There is a peel or paddle standing by the wall. What is it made of and why? Why is it that shape?
● The main source of heat for the oven was faggots of wood, coal or charcoal. How would you know when it was hot enough? (Pebbles that changed colour when heated could be used or a stick was scraped along the bottom; if sparks flew it was hot enough.)
● Metal containers were used for bread or pastries rather than wooden ones. Why might that be?
● Bowls with damp cloths on them probably have dough set to rise in them. Why are they placed above the oven?
● The cloth by the peel was used to wipe out the oven after the embers had been raked out. It was usually sopping wet. Why might this be used? (It created steam that contributed to a moister loaf.)
● Scales were needed to weigh the ingredients.

● Blue painted walls were said to deter flies. Does this really work and why might people want to deter flies?

● Ovens were used for all sorts of baking as well as bread – the oven cooled slowly and so could be used for a number of different types of baking.

● Ovens in big houses were large as they had to provide bread, cakes and pastries for a large number of people. They took a long time to heat up. Loaves were baked in big batches.

● The process involved considerable time and effort.

Note down some key points on the board during the discussion, in answer to the questions above. Encourage the children to ask further questions and consider some questions of your own such as:

● What was it like to work in a bakehouse?

● When would the bakehouse be most busy?

20 mins Development

Split the children into groups or pairs and distribute copies of photocopiable pages 131 and 132. Explain that on photocopiable page 132 they must write down their impressions of the image on photocopiable page 131 before moving on to answer the next questions.

10 mins Plenary

Invite the children to give oral feedback on something they have found out about bakers in the past.

Differentiation

Give adult support to less able children so that they can be part of a group response through shared writing, when they complete photocopiable page 132.

Assessing learning outcomes

Can the children complete the following statements: *I would / would not have liked to be a baker because… Bakers were important because…* Can they list and describe three other things they have found out about breadmaking or bakers in the past?

ICT opportunities
Use a desktop publishing program to make a poster to demonstrate the different stages of breadmaking and to label the equipment used in a bakery. Add illustrations from clip art.

Follow-up activity
Make bread using an old recipe, an activity which could run concurrently with the main activity, using additional adult support.

How has breadmaking changed?

Background information

Much of the breadmaking process is now mechanised. This allows large amounts of bread to be baked much more quickly. An ordinary loaf needs about three-quarters of an hour in the oven these days. Some larger plant bakeries now use travelling bakeries. The dough is placed in moulded tins at one end of a moving belt. As the belt moves very slowly through the oven, the bread is baked and the finished loaf emerges from the other end. It must be cooked slowly or the bread is spoilt. The heat of the oven steams the inside and bakes the outside into a hard crust. After cooling, the loaves are sliced and wrapped before being dispatched in bakery vans.

A new process being developed at the moment is baking by high-frequency heat.

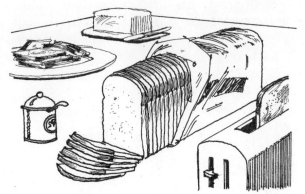

Learning objective
Make distinctions between aspects of their own lives and those of past times.

Lesson organisation
Teacher-led introduction; whole-class demonstration and plenary.

Breadmaking through the ages

Vocabulary
machines
mixer
dough hooks
electricity
steam
process
conveyer belt
dispatch
delivery
packaging

ICT opportunities
● Use *Hyperstudio*, and a digital camera if available, to record the visit. This could be used as a reference by other classes.
● Write an account of the visit for a class or school newspaper, using a desktop publishing programme.

Follow-up activities
● Research the background of well-known bakery firms, for example Hovis, or local bakery firms.
● Look at delivery methods in the past, such as bakery vans and hand carts.

With this process a loaf can be produced in three minutes. Although the result is not as good, as the bread has no crust, the produce could be most useful in cases of international emergencies when a large amount of bread would be needed very quickly. Bread still remains a staple part of diet in most parts of the world.

What you need and preparation
Arrange a visit to a local supermarket bakery or to a local baker. Collect some pictures or posters of modern bakeries. You will also need: a pre-prepared worksheet (see 'Development'); board or flip chart; writing materials.

What to do

20 mins Introduction
Talk to the children about the process of breadmaking (weigh ingredients, mix, knead, prove, knock back, prove, bake). Ask:
● How long does this take if we do it all by hand?
● What if we have a large amount of bread to make? Is this the best way to go about it?
  Allow the children to suggest alternatives, and collate and record their ideas on the board.
  Now show them the pictures or posters of modern bakeries. What is happening and how do they know? Tell the children that on their visit to the bakery they will be looking at the process for making large amounts of bread – how the machines are used and the differences between baking now and in the past.

45 mins Development
Visit the bakery, allowing the children to complete the worksheet you have previously prepared while they are there, if possible. The worksheet could take the following format:
● Find three things that are the same as breadmaking in the past.
● Find three things that are different from breadmaking in the past.
● Use three words to describe the modern bakery.
● Draw a picture of part of the breadmaking process.

10 mins Plenary
Discuss the children's original ideas about the modern bakery. How do these compare with the reality? What did the children find most surprising? What did they think was most interesting? (Try to exclude any tasting they might have done!)

Differentiation
Provide adult support for less able children to record their responses on the photocopiable sheet.

Assessing learning outcomes
Were the children able to identify at least three differences between breadmaking in the past and in the present? Were they able to give explanations for these changes?

Periods beyond living memory

The National Curriculum encourages children to investigate both the more familiar immediate past and that of long ago. It is important that children understand what is expected of them when they come to undertake the period studies of Key Stage 2. Looking at the way of life of people in the more distant past allows children to develop the skills that will be needed in the next key stage. The choice of period is extremely wide, allowing schools to select those most appropriate for their specific needs.

The unit 'Castles' gives children the opportunity to consider the reasons for castles being built and to understand how they were defended. It has strong links with geography, design and technology, and science, and also has a selection of stories that can be used in the Literacy Hour. The medieval period is rich in visual imagery that helps capture children's imagination.

The 'Stone Age' in what is now Britain would cover a period of thousands of years, in the course of which conditions, climate and people changed drastically. The activities in this unit are based on a time roughly at the end of the Mesolithic, just before the introduction of agriculture (about 6000 years ago). Study of such early periods has a chequered history in schools. At one time 'Cavemen' was a standard topic in infant schools but it rather fell out of favour, probably due to the idea that children could not relate easily to such a remote time. Actually, young children tend to view all periods beyond their own memories as equally remote ('Can you remember the dinosaurs, Mum?'). The fact that life in the Stone Age contrasts so very much with their own can make differences, and the reasons for people acting as they did, clearer and easier to discuss.

The term 'cavemen' has not been used for several reasons. Firstly it is not very accurate. People have lived in caves throughout history, but only in places where suitable caves could be found (often in limestone areas). Cave dwelling seems to have been popular in periods of colder climate (like the last Ice Age) but even then people would have to have been using other forms of shelter. The second reason is that 'cavemen' sound rather subhuman, whereas we shall be talking about people with brains and intelligence similar to our own, but living in a different way. Lastly, most schools will find it difficult to visit a suitable cave in order to give children that concept.

The problems and opportunities for humans like us of living in a natural environment will be dealt with in the unit 'Life in the Stone Age', with a few elements 'borrowed' from other times and places that might reasonably have existed at that time. People lived by *gathering* wild plant food and *hunting* wild animals. They moved periodically to take advantage of new food supplies, so there were no permanent settlements. This was certainly not aimless wandering, but rather a rotation around different bases appropriate to different times of the year. Survival depended on knowing one's environment very well. There are hunter-gatherers today in some parts of the world, such as Australia, South Africa and South America, and we can deduce something about life in the British Stone Age from their ways. We also have the archaeological record. This consists of those artefacts or other traces that have survived from that time. In practice, flint tools form the largest part of this record but that does not mean that everything in those days was made of stone, only that stone lasts very well, while wood, natural fibre, leather and so on do not.

Castles in the Middle Ages

Enquiry questions	Learning objectives	Teaching activities	Learning outcomes	Literacy links	Cross-curricular links
Why was the castle built here?	● Begin to realise that there are reasons why people in the past acted as they did.	Discuss what a castle is and why people built them. Look at possible sites for a castle. Decide what would be the optimum site referring to the different reasons for building castles.	Children: ● explain why castles were built on particular sites	Label a site for different properties using arrows; drawing and labelling a diagram.	Numeracy: data handling – use a numerical chart to decide the optimum site. Geography: land use – what relationship is there between the site and the terrain?
What was the castle like?	● Demonstrate factual knowledge and understanding of aspects of the past beyond living memory.	Use plans and photographs of different castles. Decide what different parts and rooms there were within the walls. Come together to make a class plan of a typical castle.	● name different parts of the castle and explain why they are situated where they are	Gather words to do with castles. Look at the etymology of words specific to castles, such as *pantry* and *buttery*.	Numeracy: measuring activity looking at the size of different features of castles. Design and technology: making models of castles from plans.
Who worked in the castle?	● Identify ways in which the past is represented. ● Answer questions from sources.	Introduce different characters who might have worked within the castle. Research further using secondary sources.	● introduce themselves as particular characters, explaining what they do and what part of the castle they work in ● draw and write up a description	Use a writing frame to produce descriptions of a character based on research.	Numeracy/geography: data handling – colour-code different parts of the castle and map out who would use them. Art: look at the decoration and design of different areas of the castle.

Enquiry questions	Learning objectives	Teaching activities	Learning outcomes	Literacy links	Cross-curricular links
What was life like for the children of the lord?	● Find answers from sources that go beyond simple observations – begin to make deductions.	Use pictorial sources to try to understand how the rich lived.	● identify different aspects of the life of a wealthy child and justify their answers	Shared story writing about the life of the lord's daughter .	Art: iluminated letters and medieval art.
What happened when the castle was attacked?	● Begin to understand why castles were attacked and the effect this had on people's lives.	Split into two groups – attackers and defenders. Problem solving activity. Where were there weaknesses and how could these be attacked or defended?	● give reasons for attacks on castles ● consider the effect that these attacks would have	Shared reading of accounts from contemporary sources of an attack.	Science/design and technology: forces – look at projectile machines and siege engines PE: look at how forces on buttresses work.
How did the people celebrate their victory?	● Select and combine information from a variety of sources. ● Communicate their findings in a variety of ways.	Set up the classroom for a medieval banquet or feast. Role-play victory celebrations.	● recognise different features of the feast and explain what they liked.	Shared poetry writing using a contemporary account.	Music: listen to medieval music. Design and technology: food – make some confectionery. PE: learn a simple dance.

Castles in the Middle Ages

Why was the castle built here?

1 hour 10 mins

Learning objective
Begin to realise that there are reasons why people in the past acted as they did.

Lesson organisation
Whole-class, teacher-led discussion; individual development; whole-class plenary.

Background information

Although there is a long tradition of defensive structures in Britain, from neolithic camps through to Celtic hill-forts and Scottish brochs, a castle generally means to us the Norman stone castle. When William the Conqueror took the throne he disinherited many English landowners and handed over vast tracts of the country to repay his foreign supporters for their help. These great lords in their turn shared out their domains with the knights who supported them. All this created a situation in England where French-speaking lords ruled English and Danish-speaking peasants. Each Norman lord would need a small private army of Men at Arms to keep control of his lands. Stone castles grew from the original wooden motte and bailey defensive structures. They were built as strong points to dominate the conquered country. As the Middle Ages progressed, civil war was a fairly regular occurrence. When Henry I died, 'God and his saints slept' while a barbaric conflict decided whether Matilda or Stephen would rule. The period we call the Middle Ages ended with the 30-year War of the Roses. In these wars, great lords took and changed sides quite regularly, their castles being their bases and defensive positions.

The castle was above all designed to withstand siege. It had to be a self-sufficient community with water supplies and stores as well as strong walls and armaments.

More information can be found in the following books: *A Teacher's Guide to using Castles* by Tim Copeland (English Heritage), *Learning from Country Houses* by Chistopher Culpin (National Trust), *Chronicles of the Age of Chivalry*, edited by Elizabeth Hallam (Bramley Books) and *Most Wise and Valiant Ladies* by Andrea Hopkins (Collins & Brown), *The Pastons in Medieval Britain,* edited by Martyn Whittock (Heinemann). Useful children's books are *What Were Castles For?* by Phil Roxbee Cox (Usborne), *The Best-ever Book of Castles* by Philip Steele (Kingfisher Books) and *Medieval Life* by John Guy (Addax). These are just a selection of what is available.

What you need and preparation

Prepare a large sketch map showing physical features such as hills, a river and woods – there should be several possible sites for a castle. Find images of different types of castles (include a medieval stone castle such as Bodium) and construct a timeline, with illustrations of castles at hand to add to it. You will also need: photocopiable pages 133 and 134; vocabulary sheets or flash cards; board or flip chart; writing and drawing materials.

Vocabulary
castle
site
motte and bailey
medieval
period
hostile
facilities
fortification
physical features

What to do

40 mins **Introduction**

Introduce the topic of castles. What do the children understand by the word *castle*? Collate answers and definitions on the board. Children may think of fairy tale castles as portrayed by Disney as well as others from films such as *Chitty Chitty Bang Bang* and earlier models like motte and bailey or hill-fort examples.

Look at images of different castles. Include some images from different parts of the world that might not fit with a vision of a medieval castle as found in England and Wales. Now produce an image of a medieval stone castle such as Bodium or Dover.

Castles in the
Middle Ages

Refine the answers on the board until you arrive at a definition that fits this type of castle; you will need to include features such as stone walls, battlements, drawbridge, moat, towers, gatehouse and so on. Tell the children that this is the type that you are going to investigate. Ask them:

- Why do you think that castles were built?
- Does the type of architecture tell us anything? (Point out defensive features such as thickness of walls and moats.)
- What sort of places were castles? (Castles were strong places that were meant to defend their inhabitants and dominate the local area.)

Look at the large sketch map. Suggest to the children that they might like to help decide on a site for a new castle.

- What sort of thing do we need to consider if we are going to build a home in a hostile place?
- What facilities would we need?

List the things that need to be considered (see the table below for suggestions). Decide with the children on whether there are some that are more important than others (for defence, height would be a priority, for example). Explore several possible sites for a castle and compile a table with the children, such as:

ICT
opportunities
● Data handling: enter data about the factors relating to different sites onto a spreadsheet type program. Ask questions and use graphics (for example, graphs) to present and analyse answers.
● Research sites of different castles using the Internet.

	Good Visibility	Height	Water	Track/road	Fuel source	Level ground
Site A	*	o	*	**	***	***
Site B	**	***	*	*	**	**

Key

*** very easily available   * not easily available

** available   o not available at all

Use the table to help you decide which site to develop, after weighing up the different attributes. Add an illustration of a castle to the map, placing it on the chosen site.

(20 mins) Development
Give out copies of the simplified map on photocopiable page 133 and the table on photocopiable page 134. Ask the children to decide on a site for their own castle, choosing from the sites marked A to E. Explain that they should then fill in the table and try to give three reasons for placing their castle in that particular position.

(10 mins) Plenary
Take the children through the timeline you have prepared, putting on the different castles that belong to different periods of time. Point out the type of castle that you have focused on in the activity, to enable children to identify its place in time in history.

Follow-up activities
● Watch extracts from videos such as 'Medieval Realms' in *Flying Through History* (*Eureka* series).
● Watch extracts from English Heritage videos such as *Pickering Castle*. Focus on why the settlements developed where they did when they did.
● In an additional session, investigate how castles were built and look at the techniques, materials and skills used.

Differentiation

Give adult support to the lower-ability group, encourage a shared response and provide the children with pictorial vocabulary sheets.

Assessing learning outcomes

Can the children give three reasons to explain why castles were built on particular sites (with reference to factors that needed to be considered)?

Castles in the
Middle Ages

1 hour What was the castle like?

Learning objective
Demonstrate factual knowledge and understanding of aspects of the past beyond living memory.

Lesson organisation
Group activity for investigative task; teacher-led whole-class development and plenary.

Background information
Castles grew up around the need to protect the living quarters of the lord. Often these were in the form of a stone keep or tower that replaced the original wooden motte and bailey construction. The lord's quarters would be in the most strongly defended central portion. Around those living quarters would be the other important rooms, the chapel, the great hall and the solar. Service rooms such as kitchens and stables would be within easy reach of the important public rooms but not always linked to them. A source of water was also an important consideration in building a castle. Sometimes the central keep could be entirely self-sufficient if necessary. Around these living areas a huge defensive ring of stone was constructed, usually with only one strongly defendable point of entry – the gatehouse. Castle walls were built to allow defenders to keep out attackers. They included towers and defensive positions often with a moat or ditch around them. Each castle was slightly different in design, allowing for the differences of location and building techniques and materials and in order to make it more difficult to conquer.

General information on castles and how they work can be found on the following websites:
www.castles-of-britain.com
www.castlesontheweb.com
www.castlewales.com/home.html
www.aboutscotland.co.uk/castles/castles.html
www.castles.org
www.users.globalnet.co.uk/~ctaylor/castles.htm

Vocabulary
moat
crenellations
drawbridge
pantry
buttery
great hall
courtyard
fortifications
tower
battlements
solar
chapel
keep
barbican
ditch
bakehouse
stables
inner or outer ward

What you need and preparation
Find some images of different medieval castles. You will also need: photocopiable page 135; vocabulary sheet with definitions of different areas (use the vocabulary list, left); large sheets of paper to record ideas; large laminated set of cut-out shapes (with Blu-Tack or magnetised), such as gatehouse, chapel, keep, towers and so on with labels; writing and drawing materials.

What to do

30 mins Introduction
Explain that the children will be starting off the activity with an investigative task. Split them into groups and give out copies of photocopiable page 135. Allow ten minutes for the children to investigate the plan and try to decide what the different parts of the castle could be used for – whether for defence or as living areas. The group must then try to design their own castle and label the different areas, drawing their design onto a large sheet of paper. They should also include a key to their symbols. Either nominate or allow each group to select a spokesperson to report back to the class their group's solution to the task.

20 mins Development
Examine the different group solutions. Is there anything that is common to all of them? On a large sheet of paper, build up a class plan for a medieval castle. Add laminated features and labels to the basic plan of the walls. Discuss why the different features are located in specific areas and how the different areas are interrelated. You may find that children have additional features that have not been considered, such as toilets or a well. Ask:
● Where is the great hall in relation to the lord's living rooms, the kitchens and the chapel?
● Which part of the castle has the most fortification and why might this be?
● Which is the most important part of the castle and how do you know this?

ICT opportunities
Use a geography mapping program to record a class plan of a castle.

(10 mins) Plenary

Pick out features which affect the positioning of rooms, such as the need for defence, heat or water, whether rooms are for public or private use. This could be recorded by colour-coding the plan or adding some symbols to designate different features. Begin to discuss who might use the different areas.

- Where would the lord live?
- Where would the soldiers go?
- How would the food get from the kitchen to where it would be eaten?

Differentiation

Rather than asking children to label their own castle (see photocopiable page 135), provide them with a pre-drawn one and let them label different areas with guidance from an adult helper. A higher-ability group can research the keep and the different rooms and how they were arranged.

Assessing learning outcomes

Can the children name different parts of the castle and explain why they are situated where they are?

Follow-up activities

● Carry out some fieldwork on the site of a castle, with practical investigation of the site and the different areas. Encourage the children to think about the purpose of each area.
● Plot the different areas within the castle and contrast usage, location, decoration and so on. Compile a chart to draw conclusions about how the castle functioned.

(1 hour) Who worked in the castle?

Background information

Castles needed to be self-sufficient and so were like a small village enclosed within defensive walls. They kept large households which tended to have specific areas of responsibility. The three main areas were the garrison or those responsible for defence; those charged with the running of the household, usually divided into indoor and outdoor areas; and those with direct responsibility for the lord's personal household. Each of these areas had their own specific hierarchy which were ultimately responsible to the lord of the manor. The lord was the most powerful of all and could manage his vassals as he saw fit. When the lord was absent from his holding for one reason or another, the running of the castle was left to a steward or the lord's lady.

Useful websites are:

www.castles-of-britain.com/castle32.htm

www.millersv.edu/~english/homepage/duncan/medfem/domestic.html

What you need and preparation

Prepare some images of different characters who would have lived in the castle – lord and lady of the manor, chamberlain, cook and so on. You will also need: photocopiable page 136; information books; board or flip chart; paper; writing and drawing materials.

What to do

(20 mins) Introduction

Ask the children who they think was the most important person in the castle. Introduce the lord and lady of the manor, showing the children the pictures of these characters. Ask who else would be living in the castle. (Link this to the previous session on investigating the different areas of the castle buildings.) Who would be needed to make the castle work? Brainstorm with the children who they think might have lived in the castle. Show them the images of different characters and discuss what sort of clues they might look for, such as clothing, belongings and so on. Collate their answers on the board.

Learning objectives

● Identify ways in which the past is represented.
● Answer questions from sources.

Lesson organisation

Whole-class, teacher-led introduction; pairs research activity; individual work within whole-class plenary.

Vocabulary

lord
lady
steward
reeve
cook
priest or chaplain
blacksmith
chamberlain
minstrel
pantler
butler
groom
armourer
garrison
huntsman
ladies-in-waiting
manor

Castles in the
Middle Ages

Development

20 **mins** Allocate different characters to the children (see the vocabulary on the previous page for examples of possible characters) and give them a writing frame to structure the task – this is provided on photocopiable page 136. Encourage the children to use information books for reference; they can work in pairs to research their character.

Plenary

20 **mins** Let the children take turns to introduce their characters to the rest of the class. Check how well these match the characters listed on the board in the initial brainstorm.

Now place the images of the characters, shown to the children during the brainstorm, either in a pyramid, to demonstrate the hierarchy, or in the relevant areas of the castle plan. A plan of the keep could also be used, with the characters put next to or in the relevant rooms.

Differentiation

Provide less able groups with simplified texts when they are carrying out their research, and encourage them to work on a group response, with adult support, when they are completing photocopiable page 136.

Invite more able children to research further, using the Internet, or to research the history of a prominent local family.

Assessing learning outcomes

Can the children introduce their characters, explaining who they are, what they do and what part of the castle they work in?

① hour What was life like for the children of the lord?

Background information

The lives of the rich were not as grievously hard as those of the poor, although they were liable to suffer from the same childhood diseases. Children were expected to do as their parents wished and many were married young for dynastic purposes. The different genders were educated differently as their responsibilities would be different as they grew older. Girls were expected to learn how to keep and manage a household, being responsible for overseeing the duties of the household staff and having direct control of the still room, the linen cupboard and often the household accounts. Girls were educated at home by their mothers or the women of the house. Boys would expect to be more involved with the wider world. They could expect to be educated by the priest or even a private tutor. They needed to know about warfare and have personal skill at arms. They might also be taught how to read and write and the etiquette needed to function in polite society. They could well be fostered in another household as a squire before beginning their training as a knight.

What you need and preparation

Collect together a series of images showing rich children engaged in different activities – see *Chronicles of the Age of Chivalry*, edited by Elizabeth Hallam (Bramley Books), *Most Wise and Valiant Ladies* by Andrea Hopkins (Collins & Brown) and *The Pastons in Medieval Britain*, edited by Martyn Whittock (Heinemann). Relevant children's books are *What Were Castles For?* by Phillip Roxbee Cox (Usborne), *The Best-ever Book of Castles* by Phillip Steele (Kingfisher) and *Medieval Life* by John Guy (Addax). Postcards from museums which have medieval exhibits, or illustrations from the medieval Book of Days would also be useful. Prepare some pictures of different categories

– type of clothing, education, activities inside the castle, activities outside, sleeping quarters, living areas, food and so on – for the children to investigate various elements of the life of the rich. You will also need: paper; writing materials; photocopiable page 137 (for follow-up activity).

What to do

Introduction
20 mins Begin with a hot-seating session in which you take on the role of the son or the daughter of the lord. Explain to the children that they should pretend that you are the character and ask you questions about what life is like in the castle. Give them some ideas of what areas they could ask about, for example the type of clothes worn, activities that form part of the day, the food eaten. Encourage the children to take notes on the main points when you are giving your answers (these will be useful in the plenary).

Development
25 mins Split the children into groups, and give each group a series of pictures to sort into different categories – food, play, sleeping and so on. These will give some idea of what life was like for rich children. Ask each group to choose a spokesperson to report back to the rest of the class to explain what they have found out from their pictures.

Plenary
15 mins Tell the children to write down individually three things they have found out about:
- the life of a lord's son, *or*
- the life of a lord's daughter.

Differentiation
Allow less able children to use a prepared writing frame or cloze passage when they do the task in the plenary. Ask a high-ability group to research further the people involved with rich children's lives, such as a tutor or dancing master.

Assessing learning outcomes
Can the children identify different aspects of the life of a wealthy child and justify their answers, such as *I think... because...*?

Follow-up activity
Contrast the life of the rich and poor, linking the last two sessions and referring to photocopiable page 137.

What happened when the castle was attacked?
1 hour 10 mins

Background information
Castles were constantly threatened with attack. They were built as part of a strategic defence and to help the Norman conquerors to control their occupied land. As a consequence of this, castle defences became more and more elaborate and sophisticated as siege engines and other attack weapons became more effective. The aim of the castle was to hold out until the attackers gave up and went away or until the castle was relieved by friendly troops coming to their aid. The aim of the attackers was to get into the castle to take control of it and the surrounding land or to try to starve the defenders out. Often a powerful lord would own several properties and so would not always be 'home' when the castle was attacked. It may have been the steward who was then responsible for the defence of the site. Often, however, this role would fall on the lady of the castle if she were at home. Many medieval lords relied on their wives to defend their properties, and women played a crucial and sometimes active role in medieval warfare.

Learning objectives
Begin to understand why castles were attacked and the effect this had on people's lives.

Lesson organisation
Teacher-led, whole-class introduction followed by group work and whole-class plenary for feedback.

CHAPTER 3
PERIODS BEYOND LIVING MEMORY

Castles in the Middle Ages

Vocabulary
moat
drawbridge
portcullis
garrison
battlements
siege
catapults
siege engine
attack
defence
projectile

For further information see *Chronicles of the Age of Chivalry*, edited by Elizabeth Hallam (Bramley Books) and websites www.pbs.org/wgbh/nova/lostempires/trebuchet/race.html and http://homepage.mac.com/mfeinberg/castles.html

What you need and preparation
You will need: photocopiable pages 138 and 139; pictures of attackers or defenders in action; paper; board or flip chart; writing materials.

What to do

(20 mins) Introduction
Split the children into two groups and explain that one group must imagine that they are defending a castle and the other group attacking it. Ask the defenders:

● What sort of things do you need to store?
● Are there any areas where you cannot see the attackers? What can you do about it?
Ask the attackers:
● How can you try to destroy the castle stores so that the defenders have to give in?
● Where would be the best place to use your different siege engines?

Discuss different options in response to the questions and encourage the children to think about reasons for the attack of a castle (to gain land) and the effect it would have on people's lives (fear, disruption and lives lost).

(40 mins) Development
Distribute copies of photocopiable pages 138 and 139 to each group and write the following questions on the board:

● Why is a castle attacked? (Ask the children to tick the correct statements on photocopiable page 138. Possible answers are 1. f or p; 2. p; 3. t; 4. p; 5. t; 6. t; 7. t or p; 8. f; 9. t; 10. f.)
● Why is it important to defend a castle?
● Choose two pictures of weapons that you think would be the best for attackers to use. Write a sentence to explain why you have chosen them.
● Write down three things that you think would happen when a castle is attacked.

(10 mins) Plenary
Invite the children to provide some feedback on the answers that they gave to the questions in the development session.

Differentiation
By outcome. More able children could give additional reasons for a castle being attacked when they are working through photocopiable page 138.

Assessing learning outcomes
Can the children give reasons for attacks on castles and consider the effect that these would have?

How did the people celebrate their victory?

(1 hour 15 mins)

Background information

The lord used the great hall to entertain his guests and to demonstrate his importance and social standing. The more elaborate the feast, the greater the lord's prestige. Prized possessions such as linen, tapestries and silver were displayed as a sign of the wealth of the household. Rich food was intricately prepared and fantastically decorated. It was delivered to the high table with great ceremony including fanfares of music. The lord, his guests and important members of his household sat at the dais and were served first. One of the duties of the squires was to wait on the high table, serving food and pouring wine. Delicacies such as spiced wines and salt were only available for the use of those at the high table. The lord, and perhaps the lady, of the household would have had chairs, but most other guests would have sat at stools or benches. Minstrels entertained the guests with songs and storytelling, usually at the end of the meal.

What you need and preparation

Set up the classroom as the hall, placing a class collage or some material behind the 'high table' as a tapestry. Have to hand the relevant materials to make the place-settings, food and decorations for the tables, and hats and costumes. Excellent illustrations as well as recipes can be found in *The Medieval Cookbook* by Maggie Black (British Museum Press) and *The Art of Dining* by Sara Paston-Williams (The National Trust). Arrange for some medieval music to be played during the activity.

What to do

20 mins Introduction
Explain to the children that they are going to hold a medieval feast. Point out the arrangements that have been made to the room and show them your plan of the great hall. Ask them to think about what the great hall would have looked like and what sort of activities the people would have taken part in. What would have been needed for the feast? Look at illustrations of banquets in the books you have selected for ideas of dress, decoration and type of food.

50 mins Development
Now let the children prepare various resources that would be needed for the feast, for example some marchpane sweets; hats or costumes; decorations for the table. For the food, use medieval recipes such as ones for pine nut candy (see *The Medieval Cookbook*) and red and white gingerbread (see *The Art of Dining*) for the sweets.

Split the children into different groups – lord, guests and household; those living in the castle; servants and squires. Talk to each group about what their role will be. Keep a central role for yourself so that you can direct the role-play.

Play the music and enter the room with ceremony, the children having taken their places for the feast. Role-play the feast.

5 mins Plenary
Talk about the elements of the activity the children enjoyed most. During the role-play did they appreciate what it would be like to hold a celebratory feast in the great hall?

Assessing learning outcomes

Can the children recognise different features of the feast and explain what they liked, for example by drawing an episode from the feast and commenting on how they enjoyed it? (This can be carried out in a later session, after the role-play.)

Learning objectives
● Select and combine information from a variety of sources.
● Communicate findings in a variety of ways.

Lesson organisation
Teacher-led, whole-class introduction followed by group tasks and whole-class plenary.

Vocabulary
dais
great hall
banquet
feast
celebration
entertainment

ICT opportunities
Use a multimedia programme such as *HyperStudio* to record the children's experiences of the banquet – start with a scene of the great hall and have buttons to take children to different cards, such as people at the high table, music at the feast, duties of the squire.

Life in the Stone Age

Enquiry questions	Learning objectives	Teaching activities	Learning outcomes	Literacy links	Cross-curricular links
What was it like in the Stone Age?	● Gain understanding of aspects of the past beyond living memory. ● Recognise that their own lives are different from the lives of people in the past.	Read the story 'Bearcub and the Blackberries'; children categorise aspects of their own lives and Bearcub's.	Children: ● distinguish between aspects of their own lives and aspects of life in the Stone Age by placing foods in the right categories		Geography: enquiry into the local natural environment.
What happened in Bearcub's adventure?	● Place events in order.	Read the story 'Bearcub's adventure'; children place events in the story in sequence.	● sequence the story of Bearcub's adventure	Discuss familiar story themes (such as dream adventures) and link them to own experiences.	Geography: enquiry into the local natural environment.
How did people paint in the Stone Age?	● Show knowledge and understanding of aspects of the past beyond living memory.	Read the story 'Bearcub paints a picture'; practical lesson making and using natural painting materials in the style of cave art.	● distinguish between aspects of their own lives and aspects of life in the Stone Age ● suggest other appropriate Stone Age materials		Art: investigating a range of materials; differences and similarities of work from a different time in history.

Enquiry questions	Learning objectives	Teaching activities	Learning outcomes	Literacy links	Cross-curricular links
How did people entertain themselves in the Stone Age?	●Place events in order. ●Communicate historical knowledge through dance and drama.	Practical PE activity sequencing events in the story and communicating through music and movement.	●sequence the story of Bearcub's adventure and communicate the story through dance	Understand time and sequential relationships in stories – what happened when. Prepare and tell stories individually and through role-play in groups.	PE: combine movements in a sequence. Music: exploring sounds and rhythms and expressing ideas in a sequence of sounds.
How do we know about the Stone Age?	●Observe and handle sources of information to answer questions about the past.	Museum visit or museum outreach activity looking at stone tools.	●answer questions or form hypotheses about the past by examining archaeological evidence	Making a class glossary. Writing non-chronological reports.	
Would you have liked to have lived in the Stone Age?	●Show understanding of aspects of the past beyond living memory.	Discussion and use of writing frame.	●demonstrate understanding of aspects of life in the Stone Age, firstly by correctly referring to aspects mentioned in discussion and secondly by giving reasoned opinions for whether they would like it.		

Life in the Stone Age

① What was it like in the Stone Age?
hour

Learning objectives
● Gain understanding of aspects of the past beyond living memory.
● Recognise that their own lives are different from the lives of people in the past.

Lesson organisation
Teacher-led discussion with the whole class; individual development; whole-class plenary.

Vocabulary
Stone Age
hunting
gathering

Follow-up activity
Children can start to research the animals and plants mentioned in the story, and this work could go hand in hand with a study of the local natural environment. A large wall display that portrays the area of the school in the Stone Age would be a good way of communicating the results.

What you need and preparation
Collect together some food that would have been eaten in the Stone Age period – blackberries, nuts and so on. Have a few pictures of other foods that would have been eaten at that time, such as shellfish; minibeasts would have been regarded as snacks. (Give appropriate health and safety advice to the children about *not* eating such things.) Try to find books with artists' impressions of Stone Age life, such as *Hunters of the Stone Age* (Hamlyn). Other useful books are *Food and Cooking in the Stone Age* (English Heritage) and *Wild Food* by Roger Phillips (Peerage Books). Prepare a worksheet for the children on which they can list Stone Age and modern foods – this should be simply a blank page which is separated into two sections, one headed I *like to eat* and the other *Bearcub liked to eat*. You will also need: photocopiable pages 140 and 141; board or flip chart; writing materials.

What to do

 Introduction
20 mins Read the story 'Bearcub and the blackberries' and talk about Bearcub's life. Explain that in those days there were no buildings or walls or roads or cars. Tell the children to close their eyes and try to imagine such a world. Depending on where your school is situated, you could look outside the window and pick out elements of your surroundings that *could* have been there in the Stone Age. Trees, bushes and grass might qualify, but many of those around now are not native species. Hills and rivers remain but probably looked quite different.

Discuss with the children the key idea that, in the Stone Age, people were able to get all they needed from their environment. Talk about where the children obtain their favourite foods – probably the supermarket. Then give examples of wild foods that Bearcub ate, and show the children the nuts, berries, pictures of shellfish and so on. Make a list of the foods on the board. Then add foods that children eat today to the ones listed.

Development
20 mins Now distribute the worksheets that you have prepared. Ask the children to make two lists, one of Stone Age foods and one of modern foods. Explain that they should refer to the words on the board and add their own ideas.

Plenary
20 mins Discuss some of the children's ideas. Would they have liked to have lived then?

Differentiation
Ask less able children to use pictures only to fill in the worksheet. Alternatively, let them sort foods or packaging into two sets – one for Stone Age foods, the other for modern foods.

Invite more able children to suggest what Bearcub did in the evening (for example, listening to stories around the fire) and to compare his activities with theirs today (for example, watching television and playing computer games!).

Assessing learning outcomes
Can the children distinguish between aspects of their own lives and aspects of life in the Stone Age by placing foods in the correct categories?

**Life in the
Stone Age**

① What happened in Bearcub's adventure?
hour

Background information

Obviously we do not know what stories were told in the British Stone Age. There are considerable similarities, however, between stories told by hunter-gatherers in other parts of the world. As in the case of the Australian Aborigines, great importance is often placed on dream or visionary experiences. They do not see the animals they hunt as commodities but rather as colleagues or relations who give their lives willingly, provided it is necessary. Mortal creatures and even plants and trees in this world are seen as reflections of immortal 'spirit' animals in the dream world. The story used in this activity (see photocopiable pages 142 and 143) is intended to convey some aspects of Stone Age life such as flint-knapping and hunting, but also this feeling of closeness to the natural world.

What you need and preparation

Try to obtain some large flint pebbles – often the best place to find them is on a beach. It is not advisable to experiment with knapping flint in front of the children as sharp pieces can fly about. Depending on the time of year, you could collect some leaves from the trees mentioned, or look for some pictures of them in books. You will also need: photocopiable pages 142, 143 and 144 (copies cut up for sequencing); paper.

What to do

20 **Introduction**
mins Remind the children of the story 'Bearcub and the blackberries' on photocopiable pages 140 and 141. Read the story 'Bearcub's adventure' and talk about the things that happen in it. It is important to explain why hunting was essential, not only to provide meat but also skins for clothes and tents, bones for sewing needles and so on. Show the children the flint pebbles, leaves and any other objects you have obtained that are included in the story.

20 **Development**
mins Give each child a set of jumbled up sections cut out from photocopiable page 144 and ask them to arrange the pieces of the story in the correct order. Once they have arranged the pieces of the story they can then stick them down onto a sheet of paper.

20 **Plenary**
mins Review the correct sequence of the sections of the story (photocopiable page 144) with the class.

Differentiation

Separate the words from the pictures when you are cutting out photocopiable page 144, so that more able children have to put them together before sequencing. Or you could leave out the last picture and caption and ask the children to provide them.

Assessing learning outcomes

Can the children sequence the story of Bearcub's adventure?

Learning objective
Place events in order.

Lesson organisation
Teacher-led discussion with the whole class; individual work; whole-class plenary.

Vocabulary
flint
sap
oak
ash
hazel
knapping (*chipping flint into shape*)

Follow-up activities
● Children can research the animals and plants mentioned in the story, continuing their work for the wall display started in the follow-up to the previous activity.
● Although we have no direct evidence of Stone Age music or dance in Europe, there are one or two objects that have been interpreted as musical instruments, including a whistle and castanets. Perform the story of Bearcub's adventure as a class assembly, with accompanying music on hand-made instruments (for example, cardboard tubes sealed and filled with lentils; pebbles knocked together to make a click–clack sound).

How did people paint in the Stone Age?

1 hour

Lesson organisation
Teacher-led discussion with the whole class; prepare colours in groups, individual work on paintings; whole-class plenary.

ICT opportunities
Use the Internet to carry out research.

Follow-up activity
Another form of Stone Age art, which in this case has been found in Britain in neolithic flint mines, is chalk carving. Lumps of chalk are very soft and can be incised with outlines of animals – try this out with the children, using small bits of stick.

Background information
We have practically no examples of Stone Age art from Britain. Many modern hunter-gatherers paint pictures with natural materials, and there is every reason to suppose that our ancestors did the same. The cave art from France and Spain is from an earlier period than Bearcub's but it shares many characteristics with other hunter-gatherer art and it provides impressively beautiful models.

What you need and preparation
Collect pictures of Stone Age art. You will find books in a reference library or you can get pictures from the Internet; possible sites are www.culture.fr/culture/arcnat/lascaux/en, and www.culture.fr/culture/arcnat/chauvet/en. There are also some similar lesson ideas and resources from US schools on *Mr Donn's Ancient History Page* http://members.aol.com/donnandlee/index.html, and http://members.aol.com/Tward64340/cave.htm.

Make some natural paints by using materials like clay of different colours, charcoal, powdered chalk, blackberries or other berries or fruit that stain well, mushy leaves. Mix these media into a thick paste with a little water and perhaps egg for thickening the paint. You can use feathers for painting (or children can use their fingers) and straws for spray painting. You will also need: photocopiable page 145; stones for grinding and mixing; small containers; sugar paper; aprons.

What to do

15 mins **Introduction**
Remind the children of the previous Bearcub stories and read 'Bearcub paints a picture'. Tell the children that some Stone Age pictures have survived on the walls of caves in France and Spain. Show them examples and discuss their characteristics. Ask questions such as:
● What colours did they use? (All the colours are basically earth colours.)
● What did they paint? (Nearly all the images we have are of important animals.)

Encourage the children to discuss the particular characteristics of these images, for example that they have strong black outlines and usually convey a lot of movement. Talk about the materials that Bearcub used in the story and remind them why he could not buy ready-made paints like us! Encourage the children to suggest other materials that could be used to make paints. Show them your own natural paints and demonstrate how to use them.

35 mins **Development**
Help the children to prepare their own paints in groups. To make black and white paint they should grind the charcoal and chalk in a small container, using stones. Tell them not to add too much water – beaten egg is a much better mixer, or you might cheat by using PVA glue. Let them squash the blackberries with a stone and grind the mushy leaves to make a mixture. Try feathers and sticks of charcoal to explore possible effects. Tell the children that Stone Age painters may have sprayed paint by blowing it onto a surface through animal bones or other natural tubes. Let the children experiment, carefully using drinking straws. Suggest that they paint animals that they have researched in the follow-ups to the previous two activities.

10 mins **Plenary**
Compare the effects the children have achieved with pictures of real cave art.

Differentiation
Through outcome.

Assessing learning outcomes

Can the children distinguish between aspects of their own lives and aspects of life in the Stone Age? Can they suggest other appropriate Stone Age materials?

 1 hour # How do we know about the Stone Age?

Background information

Most local museums have a collection of flint tools, as they have been found all over Britain and were in use for something like 30 000 years. The importance of flint is that it breaks easily into hard, sharp pieces that formed the best cutting tools to be had before metals came into use (in Britain bronze was introduced about 4500 years ago).

What to do and preparation

If possible, organise a trip to your local museum, to take place before the activity. You may even be able to borrow some flint tools to show to the children in the classroom. Alternatively, find some books about stone tools which show illustrations of them. You will also need: a large flint beach pebble; photocopiable page 146; paper; drawing and writing materials.

What to do

20 mins Introduction
Read the story 'Bearcub's axe' and discuss how the axe remained buried for so many years, with the earth above it changing as time moved on. Ask the children questions such as:
- How did the JCB driver know that the axe was not just a stone? (Look at the beach pebble and compare it with the axe, noting the different shapes. Point out the symmetrical shape of the worked axe and the hundreds of little chips that could not have been knocked off by accident.)
- How could you use the axe? (Pass the stone axe around so that the children can find the most comfortable way to hold it, or let them look closely at the picture of one.)
- Why did Bearcub need to cut branches? (Discuss the role of wood – for fuel and implements.)

30 mins Development
Give a picture of a flint tool, or a real object, to each group. Briefly discuss the people who made these tools. Help the children to understand that the people were as clever as they are; just using a simpler technology in a different age. Help them to realise that objects can tell us a lot about the time from which they come. By looking carefully at the tools we can form ideas about how they were made, held and used by real people, thousands of years ago. An artefact is a direct link to a past world.
Now ask the children to draw the object carefully and complete the following starter sentences:
- I think that this was made by people because I can see…
- I think this was used for…
- I think this because…

10 mins Plenary
Invite individual children to show their drawn artefact to the rest of the class. Conclude by pointing out that it is important that they do not imagine a world in which everything is made of stone; it is just that the stone survives while objects made of leather, wood and so on do not.

Differentiation

Children whose literacy skills are not strong often have good observational skills, so encourage them to take part in the discussion. Ask an adult helper to scribe their responses to the starter sentences.

Learning objective
Observe and handle sources of information to answer questions about the past.

Lesson organisation
Whole-class discussion; group or individual work on artefacts; individual presentation within whole-class plenary.

Vocabulary
flint
knapping
hand axe

Assessing learning outcomes

Can the children answer questions or form hypotheses about the past by examining the artefacts (archaeolgocial evidence)?

1 hour Would you have liked to have lived in the Stone Age?

Background information

Children are too often asked to put themselves in the place of historical characters and give opinions about historical situations without proper preparation. The intention of this activity is to assess whether the children have learned the important differences between life then and now and to find if they can understand some of the consequences of those differences. If we are to avoid a sort of 'social evolutionist' model of history – that is, one in which things just get better and better – then we need to try to bring in cons *and* pros of different periods.

What you need and preparation

Prepare a wordbank or cards with words and phrases about life in the Stone Age. You will also need: a writing frame for each child (see 'Development'); board or flip chart; writing materials.

What to do

20 mins Introduction

Sit with the children on the carpet, and review what they have learned about life in the Stone Age. Contrast each piece of information with the children's own equivalent experience, for example, *Bearcub liked blackberries, we like pizzas...*

Add to the wordbank, then widen the discussion by starting to talk about which aspects of Bearcub's life sound fun and which do not. Encourage the children to deduce other probabilities about his life, for instance that it would have been very cold in a tent in winter so he would have needed lots of animal skins to wear.

20 mins Development

Ask the children to use the following writing frame to decide whether they would have liked living in the Stone Age:

- Can you say three things that were different about life in the Stone Age?
- I would have liked living then because...
- I would not have liked living then because...

20 mins Plenary

Compare children's responses with the first part of the writing frame in which they are asked to identify three things that were different about life in the Stone Age. Gather their opinions about whether they would like to have lived in the Stone Age.

Differentiation

Encourage all children to write freely on life in the Stone Age, but allow less able children to use the wordbank on the board, together with additional stock phrases that you have provided.

Assessing learning outcomes

Do the children demonstrate understanding of aspects of life in the Stone Age, firstly by correctly referring to elements mentioned in discussion and secondly by giving reasoned opinions for whether they would have liked living at that time?

Learning objective
Show understanding of aspects of the past beyond living memory.

Lesson organisation
Teacher-led, whole class discussion; group work; whole-class plenary.

Periods within living memory

The QCA 'History, Teacher's guide Update' remarks that Curriculum 2000 has removed the requirement to progress 'from familiar situations to those more distant in time and place'. It states that the reason for this is that the new National Curriculum acknowledges the pleasure that young children take in stories about distant times. This is undoubtedly correct. History can be a 'magic carpet' which takes us to places where we can try on all sorts of new emotions and experiences. However, there are considerable advantages in a study of the more recent past. Not least of these is the fact that children's sense of the reality of history is enhanced by the presence of adults who can remember and endorse the truth of the things being studied. There will, in most cases, be more readily available evidence for recent times.

The child's sense of time and of chronology needs careful nurture. 'One hundred years' has little meaning to a young child. People, and in particular family, are living milestones for time. 'When I was little…', 'When Mummy was a little girl…', 'When Grandad was a boy…' are divisions of time that do make some sense. This presents no contradiction to the QCA statement above. There is no difficulty in talking about 'the Stone Age' to a six-year-old or even to a younger child, but you should not expect to develop their sense of chronology by doing so.

The unit 'Shopping when Granny was a little girl' is based on an aspect of everyday life familiar to all young children. It presents an opportunity to make simple then and now comparisons. The differences are quite clear and recognisable, while there is plenty of evidence still existing, not least oral accounts, to attest to their reality. Even in the children's own lifetime it is clear that changes in shopping are still occurring, which gives children a sense of historical evolution.

'Coming and going' looks at immigration in modern times, and there are suggestions in the planning grid for activities on the emigration to Canada and Australia of children from children's homes such as Barnado's. One of the most visible changes to British society within living memory is probably the development of multiculturalism. Britain has always been a popular destination for different peoples, from the Romans in 34BC to the Eastern Europeans of the present day. Different communities such as the Irish, the Huguenots, Jews and Muslims came and established themselves, contributing their own distinctive cultures to the melting pot of modern society. While some people were coming, others were going, moving north to south, from country to town and even away altogether. The clearances of Scotland saw the depopulation of vast areas of land. Within living memory there have been a number of visible comings and goings. The need for manpower in Canada and Australia created opportunities for those who wanted to seek a better life than post-war Britain seemed to offer. While the focus in this unit is on immigration from the Caribbean, it may also be appropriate for you to investigate communities that are prominent in your local area. Oral history is a feature of the unit and should allow children to be involved in gathering and investigating firsthand evidence. Care needs to be taken before undertaking a unit such as this, however. Parents and carers should be consulted beforehand in case there are any sensitive issues that need to be considered. This unit has strong links with citizenship and PSHE and should help children to understand why people came to this country. This will help them to be aware of the wider context of a mobile population that is continually changing.

Shopping when Granny was a little girl

Enquiry questions	Learning objectives	Teaching activities	Learning outcomes	Literacy links	Cross-curricular links
What was the high street like before?	● Begin to find answers from sources on the basis of simple observations.	Look at photographs of the high street and highlight main points that show that it is not a modern view of the scene.	Children: ● use a photograph to decide where a place is ● identify the clues that helped them to decide whether the photograph is old or one taken in the present day		
How has the high street changed?	● Make distinctions between aspects of their own lives and those of past times.	Walk along the high street. Take photographs at specific points. Look for changes from the old photographs. Colour-code a modern map.	● identify similarities and differences between then and now	Label a class sketch map showing points of change.	Geography: local environment; sense of place; mapping skills.
What was in these shops before?	● Use sources to ask and answer questions about the past. ● Select and combine information from sources. ● Recognise the distinction between the two periods (past and present) ● Sequence the different aspects of life.	Select several locations. Use commercial directories, advertisements and photographs to research previous owners and uses. Colour-code an old map.	● write an account of the type of shop at the location and who owned it ● recognise the distinction between past and present	Create an entry for a street directory and an advert for the shop or the service that it offered.	Design and technology: make a model of the high street. Citizenship: look at societies linked to shops or shopkeepers such as the Co-op, the Rotary Club.

Enquiry questions	Learning objectives	Teaching activities	Learning outcomes	Literacy links	Cross-curricular links
What was it like to shop for food?	● Find answers from sources that go beyond simple observations – make deductions. ● Recognise the distinction between the two periods (past and present) ● Sequence the different aspects of life.	Oral history – read or listen to an account. Role-play in groups.	● identify characteristic features of the past ● recognise the distinction between past and present	Introduction of speech marks using transcripts from an interview.	Art: shop interiors or shop signs.
How was my food packaged and stored?	● Begin to realise the reasons why people in the past acted as they did. ● Recognise the distinction between the two periods (past and present) ● Sequence the different aspects of life.	Discuss the effects of modern methods of packaging and storage. What effects do they have on people's lives? Research past methods and compare.	● compare packaging from the past and present ● suggest why changes have occurred ● recognise the distinction between past and present	Factual comparative writing that looks at the results of an investigation into past and present packaging.	Design and technology/ science: properties of different materials for packaging.
How could I pay for my purchases?	● Demonstrate factual knowledge and understanding of aspects of the past. ● Recognise the distinction between the two periods (past and present) ● Sequence the different aspects of life.	Discuss and storyboard paying for goods in old and modern stores. Compare the systems.	● explain why accounts represent the old or modern system ● recognise the distinction between past and present.	Storyboard account, ensuring the correct sequence of events.	Art: collage of shopping, old and new.

Shopping when Granny was a little girl

1 hour ## What was the high street like before?

Learning objectives
Begin to find answers from sources on the basis of simple observations.

Lesson organisation
Teacher-led demonstration; pairs or group investigative task; individual presentations within whole-class plenary.

Vocabulary
shopkeeper
parade
greengrocer/grocer
ironmonger
haberdasher
butcher
baker
florist
service
provisions
high street
market
fishmonger
newsagent
tobacconist

ICT opportunities
Scan groups of photographs into a multimedia program such as *Hyperstudio*. Children can then decide which areas they would like to highlight for others using the program. They could also give additional textual information on subsequent cards either in written form or through recording their text. If a question card is included, children could then suggest answers based on their research. This would add an interactive element to the program.

Background information
The high street, village shop or local parade of shops is a well-known feature of the children's lives. They will have spent time with their parents or carers shopping at the local supermarket and at other types of establishments, including specific retailers such as butchers, bakers and so on.

What you need and preparation
Collect together some photographs of the local area from the recent past (preferably from the 1940s and 1950s). These should show the local shops or area that the children will be researching. Enlarge them to A4 size (if they are also laminated, they can be marked with a drywipe pen when key features are being identified). Some should show interiors as well as exteriors, if possible, and there should also be images of shopkeepers and people using the shop. Collect some modern photographs of the area too – it would be helpful to have some photographs of the same shops at different times. You will also need: one large photograph, enlarged to A3 and laminated, or photocopied onto an acetate and displayed using an OHP; board or flip chart; paper; writing materials.

What to do
20 mins #### Introduction
Place the large photograph where all the children are able to see it and initiate a discussion. Can they identify the area where the photo was taken? What points of reference can the children find? Look for things such as names of roads, well-known features such as wells, bridges or monuments, local buildings that are still around such as pubs, the library or town hall, the shape of the road, the site of the green or the park. Circle them on the photograph and establish that identifying these points of reference have helped them come to a concensus about where the place is. Write on the board: *We think it is… because…*

Now encourage the children to think about whether the picture is modern or not. Does the place look the same as it does now? Using a different coloured pen, put a ring around the features that look different from the present, and write a concluding statement on the board: *We think this is an old picture because…*

Finally, ask the children to think about what the photo doesn't tell them and encourage them to suggest questions about the area that they might like to find out about. Try to guide them so that these relate in general to shops and shopping. Collate their answers on the board: *We would like to find out…*

30 mins #### Development
Give out the photographs of the local area and ask the children to work together to highlight clues that show where their picture has been taken. They must also decide if the photograph is a modern one or an old one. Ask them to write down the clues that enabled them to make their decision. They should then think of two questions to which they would like to find out the answers. (They can take turns to write their questions on the board during the course of the activity.)

CHAPTER 4
PERIODS WITHIN
LIVING MEMORY

Shopping
when Granny
was a little girl

(10 mins) Plenary

Invite the children to show their photographs to the rest of the class and to read out their conclusions. They could also explain why they have chosen to ask their particular questions, for example: *Our first question was 'How will these big cheeses be cut up?' We would like to find out about this – people will not want all of the cheese…*

Follow-up activity
Ask the children to sequence two photographs of the same place, taken in different decades, and to justify their reasoning.

Differentiation

Provide less able children with a pictorial vocabulary sheet to help them analyse the photographs and identify key features.

Assessing learning outcomes

Can the children use the photograph to decide where the place is? Can they identify the clues that helped them to decide whether the photograph was old or one taken in the present day?

How has the high street changed?

(1 hour 30 mins)

Background information

The coming of the supermarket in the late Fifties and early Sixties led to a revolution in shopping habits. The ability to visit just one shop that would carry a full range of merchandise combined with changing food storage capabilities at home meant that many people no longer had to shop daily at different high street premises. While the older generation still make use of local shops, most families now shop once a week in a large automated supermarket. This change in shopping habits has gradually been reflected in the changing face of the high street. Specific provisions stores such as butchers and fishmongers close down while empty units often become luxury-linked, such as delicatessen shops or those offering specialist skills or services, or they are taken up by charity shops. While helping children to notice these changes, you should also encourage them to reflect on why the changes have taken place and are still taking place and consider the future of the local shop as we know it.

Learning objective
Make distinctions between aspects of their own lives and those of past times.

Lesson organisation
Whole-class, teacher-led introduction and fieldwork; whole-class plenary.

What you need and preparation

This activity involves a trip to the shopping area identified in the previous activity. It is important to have walked the route you will take already and to have decided on strategic stopping points. Ensure that you have adequate adult support and, if possible, arrange for a briefing meeting with the adults before the trip. Prepare a rough sketch map of the area and include a key for colour-coding information. You will also need: photographs from the previous session; camera (digital, if available); tape recorders; paper; clipboards; writing and drawing materials.

What to do

(20 mins) Introduction

Organise the children into groups or pairs, as desired. Ensure that all children and adults understand the expectations for behaviour and the procedures that will be used once outside the school. Tell the children that on the trip they will be:

- comparing the older photographs with what is actually there now
- recording their observations both pictorially (using photographs and drawings) and verbally (using tape or written records)
- looking to see what has changed and what remains from the photographs
- categorising the shops and land use that they find on their trip by colour-coding the sketch map. You or another adult will need to list the names and addresses of the shops, for future reference.

Vocabulary
business premises
shop front
street furniture
photograph
development
land use

**Shopping
when Granny
was a little girl**

ICT opportunities
● Include clip-art illustrations, where relevant, on the classroom sketch map, and word-process captions and labels.
● Desktop publish a class book of the field trip, including scanned-in maps, photographs and drawings.
● Use a spreadsheet program to enter, store and retrieve information about the different types of shops and land use.
● Use graphics facilities to create graphs and charts.

Follow-up activity
Individually, the children can draw part of their walk and then list two or three differences and similarities that they found between an old photograph and the present day reality.

Development
1 hour Proceed with the walk, stopping at relevant points. Direct the children to look above and below eye level and to notice street furniture. Remind them to look for obvious examples of change from the photographs used in the previous session, and also to look for areas that may not have changed. Allow some of the children to take photographs of the scenes shown in the older photographs – they could even try to get the same angle to give a better point of comparison.

Encourage the children to comment on the differences between the older photographs and the present reality – adults can act as scribes or children can record observations into a tape recorder. Ask the adults to note down any significant comments or observations that the children make. In discussion, groups should collate ideas and consolidate their impressions:
● What have we found out about how the area has changed?
● Was there anything that we expected to see but didn't?
● Was there anything that surprised us?

Plenary
10 mins On return to the classroom, transfer discrete information to the large class sketch map. Land use or commercial buildings should be colour-coded and labelled. Photographs can be added at the relevant points, together with examples of the children's work.

Differentiation
By outcome.

Assessing learning outcomes
Can the children identify similarities and differences between then and now?

1 hour What was in these shops before?

Learning objectives
● Use sources to ask and answer questions about the past.
● Select and combine information from sources.
● Recognise the distinction between the two periods (past and present).
● Sequence the different aspects of life.

Lesson organisation
Teacher-led introduction followed by pairs or small-group investigative task, with report-back session.

Vocabulary
commercial
directory
source
advertisement

Background information
Local history museums and libraries have a wealth of information that can be of enormous use when trying to research the local area. Commercial directories and insurance maps or road maps can show what commercial premises were used for previously. They also often hold collections of everyday items which can include advertisements, bills and orders, and so on. Oral history can also often produce interesting titbits of information.

What you need and preparation
Take a series of shops that are still in use, albeit with different proprietors, and carry out some research to find out what types of shop they were and who the shopkeepers were previously. Try to find a shop that is still run by the same family and interview present and past shopkeepers. Make up an information pack about a particular shop for each pair or small group comprising as much as possible of the following: an entry from a commercial directory giving the name of the proprietor and the type of shop; a photograph of the shop or one like it; an advert that relates to the type of shop or the services being offered. Useful resources are *How It All Began Up the High Street* by Maurice Baren (Michael O'Mara Books) and *From the Bomb to The Beatles* by Juliet Gardiner (Collins & Brown). You will also need a sketch map of the area; secondary evidence such as simple textbooks and photographs of different types of shop; photocopiable page 147; different coloured plain stickers; writing materials.

CHAPTER 4
PERIODS WITHIN
LIVING MEMORY

**Shopping
when Granny
was a little girl**

What to do

(10 mins) Introduction

Tell the children about the items they will find in their information packs. Explain what is meant by the entry from the commercial directory. A commercial directory lists commercial properties alphabetically and geographically. It may also contain adverts relating to those shops and services. Show the children how to use the entry to find information about the shop and who owns it.

(40 mins) Development

Give the children their separate information packs and a selection of photographs and textbooks. Provide adult support, if available, for lower-ability groups (with whom you should work initially to help decode information). Work through the photocopiable sheet as a group and then allow the children to record some information individually.

(10 mins) Plenary

Select one child from each group to come to the front of the class and enter colour-coded information onto the sketch map about the type of shop that they have researched (for example, using a green sticker to symbolise a greengrocer). Use the same categories for the codes as those that would be appropriate for modern day shops. Compare the two sketch maps:

- Are there any types of shops that are found on one map and not the other?
- Are there any shops that are exactly the same type on both maps?
- Are there any shops that are still owned by the same family?
- How has the land use of the area changed? Are there more of one type or another on the different maps?

Differentiation

Ensure that adult support is provided, where necessary.

Assessing learning outcomes

Can the children use their notes on their completed photocopiable sheets to write an account of the type of shop at their address and the person who owned it? Can the children recognise the distinction between past and present?

(1 hour) What was it like to shop for food?

Background information

The end of the war in 1945 did not signal the end of rationing and the immediate return of prosperity. Serious shortages in the shops, continuing queues for basic items, austerity and rationing were depressing features of the post-war era. Rationing did not end completely until 1954! Many homes of this period did not yet have the range of household appliances that we take for granted, such as fridges. This meant that meat was often kept in a meat safe in the pantry and could not be stored for very long. Shopping therefore was done on a daily basis, although most people made use of the weekly delivery vans from the butcher, fishmonger or grocer.

ICT opportunities
- Use a desktop publishing package to design an advertisement for the shop or the services that it offered.
- Collate information about the different types of shops to compile a database and compare to that of the modern period.
- Use graphics to represent information in graphs and charts.

CHAPTER 4
PERIODS WITHIN
LIVING MEMORY

**Shopping
when Granny
was a little girl**

**Learning
objectives**
● Find answers
from sources that
go beyond simple
observations –
make deductions.
● Recognise the
distinction
between the two
periods (past and
present).
● Sequence the
different aspects of
life.

**Lesson
organisation**
Whole-class
discussion; group
and individual
development work;
whole-class
plenary.

Vocabulary
rationing
queues/queuing
delivery vans
meat safe
cold store
pantry
scullery
housewife

**ICT
opportunities**
Word-process
transcribed
comments for
display, and
include use of
speech marks.

What you need and preparation

Try to find someone who can come and talk to the children about what it was like to go shopping when they were young – that is, in the period of the late 1940s and early 1950s. (This is always far more stimulating for the children than listening to a taped account or reading a written one.) There may be a grandparent or even great-grandparent who is willing to do this. If possible, arrange for two or three people to visit your class, as this would allow children to draw parallels or recognise differences. You will need to explain the purpose of the visit and its structure to the children beforehand.

Have a tape recorder and tapes to hand, to record the interview, and possibly a camera to take photographs. Artefacts and oral history accounts of shopping in the past may also be useful. You will also need paper and writing materials.

What to do

30 mins **Introduction**
Introduce the visitor to the class and check that the tape is running and recording. Set the scene for both visitor and children. Initially, allow the visitor to talk freely about their experiences.

You may have previously discussed things that the children particularly want to find out about. Questions that deal with general areas rather than specific points are the usually most effective, and it is always important to think of open rather than closed questions. Do not be tempted to assign individual questions to particular children as this may inhibit the flow of the talk and distract the children's attention from the rest of the interview. If there are any particular areas that have not been addressed, bring these up through questions towards the end of the talk.

Show any interesting artefacts that you have obtained if the interview begins to flag and ask, for example: *Do you remember this…?* Allow the children to ask their own questions, although you may need to structure these to ensure that they are relevant.

(At a later date, allow the visitor to see that their information has been of use to you by inviting them back to see the finished display, if you make one, or giving them a copy of any work the children do. Handwritten thank-you letters are always appreciated.)

15 mins **Development**
After the visit, split the children into groups of three and allow them a short time to put together a brief role-play on shopping in the past. What shop are they going to? What time of day is it? How does the shopkeeper greet the shopper? How do they carry their shopping? How do they get to and from the shop? Circulate and monitor their work.

Now ask the children to write down three ideas, individually, showing what they think it would have been like to go shopping then.

15 mins **Plenary**
Ask the children what they have learned from the visitor. Encourage them to suggest key points that they have picked up. Ask: *What were the important things that our visitor told us?* Link their responses to the individual work that they have just done, which will help them to make evaluations. Listen to the tape of the interview and transcribe relevant comments. Select two or three comments from the tape to form part of a display or class book.

Differentiation

Scribe answers for less able children, when they are thinking about three main ideas to describe shopping in the past.

As an extension, let an able group of children set up and run their own taped interview with a different interviewee.

CHAPTER 4
PERIODS WITHIN
LIVING MEMORY

Shopping
when Granny
was a little girl

Assessing learning outcomes

Can the children identify characteristic features of the past and justify their answer? *I think it would be… to go shopping in the past because…* Can the children recognise the distinction between past and present?

(50 mins) How was my food packaged and stored?

Background information

The advent of supermarkets meant that food needed to be packaged and stored in new ways. Large fridges could now be used to keep meat and dairy produce cold. Fruit and vegetables were brought in large quantities and improved transportation meant that they could be imported from further afield. Dried and loose food such as sugar and biscuits came pre-packaged. The idea of self-service meant that people had to be able to see clearly the food that they would then select themselves. Changes in shopping habits meant that the way that food was packaged also had to change. As supermarkets grew, so more food became mass-produced and factory-packaged. Plastics and other synthetic materials allowed food to be protected for effective storage while still being attractive to shoppers.

What you need and preparation

You will need: a selection of different types of packaging for different types of food; photographs and oral history accounts of older shops pre-supermarket era; simple textbooks; a large plate of biscuits; paper; writing materials.

What to do

(20 mins) Introduction

Show the children the plate of biscuits and ask them how they think they could be packaged to be taken home without being broken. What do they need to consider? What will happen to the biscuits if they are just left out? What do we need to do to stop them breaking? How can we make them look attractive so that people will want to buy them?

Divide the children into groups and explain that they are going to investigate the packaging you have provided. Ask them to consider three areas: protection from breakages, presentation, and prevention of decay, and to give each package a mark out of five. They should then complete the statements *Modern packaging is good because…* and *Packaging in the past was good because…*

(20 mins) Development

Collate the children's marks for the packages and encourage them to report back on their findings. Try to draw some conclusions by answering the following questions:

- How effective is the modern packaging?
- Does it do the job it was designed to do?
- Does it make our lives better?

Now look at the evidence you have gathered to find out how people in the past got their purchases home. Look at textbooks, photographs and oral history accounts. Remind the children that they would not have to take their own food from the shelves as the shop assistant would serve them and wrap up their purchases for them.

Learning objectives
- Begin to realise the reasons why people in the past acted as they did.
- Recognise the distinction between the two periods (past and present).
- Sequence the different aspects of life.

Lesson organisation
Whole-class introduction with a small-group investigation; whole-class discussion followed by group investigative task in the plenary.

Vocabulary
packaging
storage
supermarket
mass production
synthetic
plastic
moulded

CHAPTER 4
PERIODS WITHIN
LIVING MEMORY

**Shopping
when Granny
was a little girl**

Follow-up activity
Research the history of different famous brands using the Internet.

Plenary
10 mins Return together as a group to answer the following questions about the type of packaging used in the past:
● What were the good points about packaging in the past?
● What were the problems that might arise when using it?

Differentiation
Ask lower-ability groups to record oral history accounts on tape. Alternatively, let them take part in shared writing with an adult helper for the factual answers they need to provide when assessing the various packaging.

Assessing learning outcomes
Can the children compare packaging from both the present and the past? Can they suggest reasons why the changes have occurred? Can the children recognise the distinction between past and present?

1 hour How could I pay for my purchases?

Learning objectives
● Demonstrate factual knowledge and understanding of aspects of the past.
● Recognise the distinction between the two periods (past and present).
● Sequence the different aspects of life.

Lesson organisation
Whole-group, teacher-led discussion; large-group development; whole-class plenary.

Vocabulary
automatic
bar code
scanner
aisle
computer
Internet
automated
itemised bill
trolley
basket
computerised till
shopwalker
ledger
cash register
counter
account
receipt
haberdashery
shop assistant
bill
customer

Background information
The impact of computers within the sphere of shopping has been enormous. Within the last 20 years, habits of generations have been completely revolutionised. Much of the shopping experience has become automated. Even the smallest of corner or village shops have computerised tills. With credit and debit cards we almost have no need to carry money. Computers are an integral feature of all facets of the shopping industry, from ordering to storage to purchase and payment. It is no longer even necessary to visit the shop itself as almost anything can now be bought over the Internet, even from outlets in other countries.

What you need and preparation
You will need: photocopiable page 148; pictures and plans of different shop interiors; blank storyboard sheets; examples of artefacts and documents such as old bills, ledgers, cash registers and so on; writing and drawing materials.

What to do
Introduction
30 mins Read and discuss the first account on photocopiable page 148. Explain any unknown vocabulary and check that the children have understood the content. Have they experienced anything like the first account? (This is probably unlikely!) How did people used to pay for their purchases? How was the bill produced? Why did it have to be entered into a ledger? What do the children

think it would be like to shop like this? What would be good about it? What would not be so good?

Read and discuss the second account. Again, explain any unknown vocabulary and check that the children have understood the content. Encourage them to talk about their own experiences of shopping today. How are goods paid for? What is better about shopping today? Do large supermarkets have any disadvantages? Are any of the children familiar with shopping over the Internet?

CHAPTER 4
PERIODS WITHIN
LIVING MEMORY

**Shopping
when Granny
was a little girl**

20 mins **Development**

Split the children into two groups, one group to work on the old system for payment and the other to do the same for the modern method. Ensure that they have photographs, pictures, plans and simple textbooks, as available. On the blank storyboards the children should sequence the process of buying and paying for goods, using words and pictures. Tell the children that it needs to be very clear whether they are representing the old or the modern system; the focus must be on features that are different, not the same.

10 mins **Plenary**

Select children to show their work to the rest of the class and discuss different features that they have included. Decide on what the benefits and drawbacks of both systems are. Include these statements as part of a finished display or class book.

Differentiation

Work with lower-ability groups to role-play either shopping in the past or shopping today before encouraging them to produce a group response storyboard. Provide them with a pictorial vocabulary sheet and adult support, if possible.

Ask high-ability groups to write a sequential written account rather than completing a storyboard with captions.

Assessing learning outcomes

Can the children explain why their accounts represent either the old or the modern system? Can they recognise the distinction between past and present?

ICT opportunities
● If Internet facilities are available investigate what is meant by e-shopping and buy a book on the topic for the classroom, if possible.
● Examine the effect of computerisation on our everyday lives.

Follow-up activities
● Set up the home corner as an old-fashioned shop.
● Either arrange a visit to a modern supermarket to look at the changes computerisation has had on the whole process or arrange for someone to come in and talk about the place that computers play in their business.
● Arrange a visit to an old, established local business. Research the history of the firm and look at old artefacts and documents, if available.

Coming and going

Enquiry questions	Learning objectives	Teaching activities	Learning outcomes	Literacy links	Cross-curricular links
Why did people come to this country from the Caribbean?	● Give reasons why people in the past acted as they did.	Use contemporary accounts and sources to investigate the different reasons for immigration.	Children: ● identify why people emigrated to Britain from the Caribbean	Design a poster to promote immigration.	Geography: investigate the Caribbean islands, looking at physical characteristics and lifestyle.
What was the *Empire Windrush* and why was it important?	● Describe some of the main events and changes.	Look at contemporary accounts and reference books to research what the *Windrush* was and why it was important.	● explain what the *Empire Windrush* was and give reasons for it being important	Look at John Agard's poem 'Windrush Welcome' and investigate how the words create effect. Look at other examples of John Agard's work.	Numeracy: look at the distance from the Caribbean to Britain and at the length of the *Windrush*'s journey; compare with a similar journey today.
What did people do when they came?	● Make distinctions between aspects of their own lives and those of past times.	Group activities to investigate the sort of jobs linked to working on buses. Compare and contrast with how buses are run today.	● recognise similarities and differences between bus travel now and in the past	Gather vocabulary linked to the topic and especially to working on buses.	Citizenship/PSHE: look at service industries and 'people who help us'.

Enquiry questions	Learning objectives	Teaching activities	Learning outcomes	Literacy links	Cross-curricular links
What was life like for those who came?	● Use sources to answer questions that go beyond simple observations to make deductions.	Oral history – use personal accounts to investigate people's initial impressions of Britain.	● make deductions and justify their ideas about what it felt like to come to this country	Illustrate and record some of the comments from the oral history accounts and make use of speech marks and speech bubbles.	Geography: compare and contrast lifestyles in Britain and the Caribbean.
Why were people leaving Britain at this time?	● Give a few reasons for and results of main events and changes.	Tell the children stories about children from the homes and discuss reasons for them being sent away – see *Lost Children of the Empire* by P Bean and J Melville (Unwin Hyman) and *Empty Cradles* by M Humphreys (Doubleday).	● suggest two reasons why the children were sent abroad	Write a letter explaining why the children were being sent away.	Citizenship/PSHE: discuss whether it was fair to send children away.
Where were they going and how did they travel?	● Select and combine information from sources.	Use archive sources to research how children travelled and where they were going. Plot the different journeys on a map.	● use two or more sources to research information about the journey	Storyboard the sequence of the journey.	Art: class collage of the ship arriving at destination (Australia could provide good scenery here).
What happened to them?	● Show how aspects of the past have been represented and interpreted in different ways.	Compare two accounts, one positive and one negative, of what happened to the children.	● explain why accounts may differ and why some felt it was a positive experience and others a negative one.	Give an account of what life was like based on eyewitness accounts.	Geography: look at the different climates and environments of Canada or Australia and think about the effect these had on people's lives.

CHAPTER 4
PERIODS WITHIN LIVING MEMORY

Coming and going

Why did people come to this country from the Caribbean?

1 hour

Learning objective
Give reasons why people in the past acted as they did.

Lesson organisation
Whole-class, teacher-led discussion followed by individual task and whole-class plenary.

Vocabulary
immigration
emigration
Caribbean
West Indies
mother country

Background information

The end of the Second World War saw victory for the Allies, but this victory had extracted an enormous price from Britain; large areas of the big cities needed rebuilding, rationing was still a feature of life, people were on the move everywhere. The work of rebuilding Britain would continue throughout the 1940s and well into the 1950s. As this rebuilding continued it produced a serious shortage of labour. Service industries began to look outside Britain for recruits. There was very little industry in the Caribbean at this time as most of the islands' economies were based on cash crops such as sugar. Growing populations and high unemployment meant that people were prepared to look beyond their islands for work. As many of the islands were still British colonies at this time it seemed reasonable for their people to respond to the recruitment drives initiated by British firms such as London Transport, the NHS and British Rail. Britain was still 'the mother country' that many of them had fought for in the war and so not surprisingly many of them were now prepared to volunteer to fill gaps in the labour market. They came for a variety of reasons – some wanted to work for specific industries, some wanted to go into other careers or study, some hoped to send money home. Many recruits were well-educated or skilled. Although the initial policy was to recruit only single men, many left families at home while they came to start a new life.

Some eyewitness accounts from the *Empire Windrush* can be found on the following websites: www.bbc.co.uk/education/archive/windrush/windrush.shtml (go to Windrush Arrivals and Word a Mout), http://learningcurve.pro.gov.uk and www.shef.ac.uk/~oip/srec/background.htm. Others can be found on the *Sun-a-Shine* website and there is information in the book *Windrush: the Irresistable Rise of Multi-racial Britain* by Mike Phillips and Trevor Phillips (HarperCollins). Alternatively you could canvass parents and grandparents of children in the school or local Afro-Caribbean societies to offer the children some personal reminiscences.

What you need and preparation

Find a map that shows both the British Isles and the Caribbean, and one that shows the Caribbean islands in some detail. You will also need: pictures of Britain and the Caribbean in the 1950s (these can be found on the PRO website *Bound for Britain* and downloaded); a large colour photograph of a street in a Caribbean town or city; a timeline marked in decades (1900–2000) and four small figures (a child, an adult, grandparent and great-grandparent); photocopiable page 149; board or flip chart; writing materials.

What to do

Introduction
30 mins
Show the children the colour picture of the Caribbean scene and ask them what they can find out about the place from the photograph:
● What sort of place is this and how do you know?
● What impression does it give you and why do you think this?
● What is the weather like and what tells you this?
● Is this place the same or different from here and how do you know?
● What is the same and what is different?

Collate the children's answers on one side of the board. Can any of the children suggest where this place might be? Have any of them been on holiday there? If so, could they explain what it was like? Avoid tales of what they did in the swimming pool; focus on weather, vegetation, buildings, colour and so on.

Coming and going

If the children do not know anything about where the place is, identify the location on the map and give a little background reference such as physical characteristics. Children may talk about family links at some point, for example *My granny comes from Jamaica and my grandad comes from Grenada.* Encourage them to become involved through personal experiences if they wish to do so. Some may not, and should not be pushed into contributing if they feel uncomfortable.

Now ask the children if the place is near to or far from where they live. (They may be able to give feedback here if they have visited the Caribbean.) Show them the map and point to the Caribbean and Britain. How could they get from one place to the other? Children will suggest planes. How else could they travel? Highlight travel by ship.

Show the children the picture of Britain in the 1950s. (Try to select one that still shows bomb damage.) Ask the same sort of questions as you did for the first picture. Collate these answers on the board and compare them with the first set. Ask the children:

● Which of these places looks most inviting?
● Why would people want to come from the warm, sunny Caribbean to this country?

Allow children to suggest possible reasons and then give some background information. Points to make include:

● Caribbean islands economies were largely agricultural – that is, based on farming.
● Prospects there were not good for work – there was lots of unemployment.
● People thought of themselves as British as Britain controlled many of the islands at this time.
● Britain was offering jobs with good prospects for the future.
● Britain was offering jobs with more money.
● Initially only single men went – women and children followed later.
● Many ex-servicemen and women had travelled the world, often going to Britain, and wanted to do so again.

ICT opportunities
Use the Internet to research the stories of the people mentioned on the photocopiable sheet. Use the BBC Windrush website. Listen to some of the stories on 'Word a Mout'.

(20 mins) Development
Give out copies of photocopiable page 149, one to each child. Read through the text together and explain any unknown vocabulary before the children record their answers.

(10 mins) Plenary
Use the timeline to demonstrate when this was beginning to happen. Work backwards, placing the figures on the timeline to show roughly the different generations. Highlight the periods that you will be looking at in the following activities – the end of the 1940s to the 1960s. Point out that we are only looking at one group of people and when and why they emigrated. Other groups came at different times and for different reasons, and people come from other countries to live in Britain at the present time.

Differentiation
Ask less able children to produce a group response to the questions on photocopiable page 149, with an adult helper acting as scribe.

Assessing learning outcomes
Can the children give reasons for people emigrating from the Caribbean to Britain?

Coming and
going

(1 hour) What was the *Empire Windrush* and why was it important?

Background information

The SS *Empire Windrush*, a former troop ship, left the Caribbean around the beginning of June 1948, bound for Britain. The fare was £28.10. The ship stopped at Trinidad, Kingston in Jamaica, Tampico, Havana, Bermuda and finally Britain. The voyage took 22 days. The ship docked in Tilbury on 22 June 1948 with 942 passengers. While there were five families on board and a number of women travelling to join husbands and families, the majority of the passengers were men. The travellers lined the rails as the ship docked. They were conspicuous with their baggy-trousered, wide-shouldered suits and distinctive trilby hats. The women were beautifully turned out with brightly coloured full-skirted dresses, hats and immaculate white gloves. They provided a vivid and enduring image that was quickly captured by the newsreels. The people who walked down that gangplank half a century ago could not have had any idea of the contributions they would be about to make to post-war British society.

What you need and preparation

Look for images of the *Windrush* arriving or West Indian immigrants. These can be found in *Windrush: the Irresistible Rise of Multi-racial Britain* by Mike Phillips and Trevor Phillips (HarperCollins) and also books such as *We Were There... 1940s* by Rosemary Rees (Heinemann), *Britain Since 1930* by Donna Bailey (Hodder & Stoughton), *Yesterday's Britain* (Reader's Digest). Information can also be found on the archive site for the *Daily Telegraph* (Electronic Telegraph Issue 1114). Look for information on the websites www.bbc.co.uk/education/archive/windrush/windrush.shtml (go to Windrush Arrivals and Word a Mout) and http://learningcurve.pro.gov.uk. You will also need: a map of the Caribbean islands; a picture of a troop ship (see *Daily Telegraph*); the timeline from the previous session; a selection of extracts of Calypso music on tape and a tape player; paper; writing and drawing materials.

What to do

(30 mins) Introduction

Remind the children of the previous session and the distance that people like Vince Reid had to travel to get to Britain from the West Indies. How long would the journey take now? How long would it have taken when Granny was a little girl?

Tell the children about the SS *Empire Windrush*. This was a ship that travelled from the Caribbean to Britain. Use the map to plot the journey of the ship around the islands. Explain that it picked up passengers at each stop. Explain that air travel was very expensive and so most people travelled by sea. This made the journey much longer. The journey took 22 days. Help the children understand this as a passage of time, for example by saying it is just under a month. What sort of things would they have done in that time? How do the children think that people passed the time? Explain that there was no television, and people amused themselves by giving concerts and boxing displays.

Show the children one of the pictures of newly arrived immigrants, and ask:

● Does this look like a modern photograph?

● How is this different?

● What do you notice about the clothes that are being worn? (Point out the number of people wearing hats or gloves and the lack of casual or sports clothes.)

Show the children when the *Windrush* voyage took place by including a little ship on the timeline. Explain that the *Windrush* was important because it was the first time that a large number of immigrants had arrived, at one time, from the Caribbean. Tell the children about how many arrived and give them information about some of the passengers.

Coming and going

(20 mins) Development

Give the children some sample pictures of newly arrived immigrants, or let them look closely at the pictures in the books. Ask them to look carefully at the clothes and think about the people's expressions. How would they have felt when they arrived at the end of their voyage? Would they have been happy, sad, frightened or excited? Give the children some paper and ask them to draw a figure, paying careful attention to the detail. This could either be drawn in monochrome tones to give the impression of a black and white photograph or with full colour, depending on the effect they want to create. As the children finish their drawings, encourage them to complete the following sentences:

- The *Empire Windrush* was…
- The *Empire Windrush* was important because…

(10 mins) Plenary

Show some of the children's drawings to the rest of the class, and read aloud a selction of their completed sentences. Ask the children for words that might describe how the people felt on arrival. Record the words, to add to a display at a later time. Listen to some of the calypso music. How does it make the children feel? What does it make them think of? Is it happy or sad music?

Assessing learning outcomes

Can the children explain what the *Empire Windrush* was and begin to think about why it was important?

ICT opportunities
Word-process various comments about the voyage for a display.

Follow-up activities
● Use drawings and a large painting of the SS *Empire Windrush* to create a display. Include a map showing the route, with a small laminated picture of the ship that children can move around. Include a timetable of events, and add information to it as the topic develops.
● Set up a listening corner, with calypso music on tapes for the children to listen to. Include books and any pictures that may be available.

(1 hour) What did people do when they came?

Background information

One of the first firms to begin direct recruitment in the West Indies was London Transport. Bus transport was one of the main forms of travel before car ownership became within the reach of ordinary families. Most people in large cities travelled to work by train, bus or the underground. These industries were labour intensive. Not only were there a large number of buses and trains being used but a huge amount of support staff were also needed. Buses were operated by a team of two people, the driver and the conductor. At this time the driver would have been a man, while the conductor, or clippie, would usually have been a woman. Inspectors regularly policed routes to ensure that all was running as it should. The fleet of buses needed regular overhauls and maintenance. Each bus was thoroughly checked at least once every three years. Canteen staff provided hot food and drink even at unsociable hours. An enormous cleaning force was needed to keep the buses pristine. Social clubs and sports facilities were provided for the workers and the union was an important feature of working life. In 1957, 87 000 people worked for London Transport in one capacity or another; today it is less that 35 000. Many services including buses and catering are operated by different firms. The faithful Routemaster buses, one of the most recognisable features of central London, are finally being phased out. Modern equivalents are solely driver operated.

More information can be found on the following websites: www.ltmuseum.co.uk (see the *Sun-a-Shine* online exhibition); www.users.globalnet.co.uk/~denny/transport/index.htm#LifeBegins (life working for LT); www.londonpostcard.co.uk (pictures of London Routemaster buses); www.londoncentral.com/ (picture of modern London bus). A large number of simple reference books that look at transport in general and buses in particular are easily available.

Learning objective
Make distinctions between aspects of their own lives and those of past times.

Lesson organisation
Teacher-led discussion; individual work and group role-play.

Coming and going

Vocabulary
bus driver
bus conductor
clippie
transport
uniform
canteen
facilities
inspector
staff
passenger

ICT opportunities
Tape-record an oral account of travelling or working on a bus with a conductor. Word-process the text and illustrate it with clip art or images downloaded from the Internet to make it into a book.

What you need and preparation

You will need: a large picture of a Routemaster bus and a picture of a modern bus to use as a contrast; recruiting poster from London Transport (see website for London Transport); a picture of a conductor and a driver; photocopiable page 150; writing materials. (Ensure that children have space for the role-play and somewhere to write when completing their photocopiable sheets.)

What to do

20 mins **Introduction**

Ask the children if they have travelled on a bus before. Select a couple of children to explain their experiences. Ask them:

● How many people were running the bus?
● Who took the money?
● How did you let the diver know when you wanted to get off?
● Was it a comfortable way to travel and why do you think this?
● Which end of the bus did you get on at?
● What did the bus look like?

Show the children the picture of the modern bus. Did their bus look similar to this (it may have been a different colour, of course). Ask if everybody has had the same experiences. Show the picture of the Routemaster bus, and ask:

● Has anyone been on a bus like this? (Some children may have visited London or another place where they have conductors on the buses and may be able to describe their experiences.)
● What was special about travelling on this sort of bus?

Now make the following points:

● The driver sat in a little box-like cab at the front of the bus but had no contact with the public. He had to climb up into his cab to get onto the bus.
● People entered at the back of the bus.
● There were no doors, but there was a pole to hang onto.
● The stairs to the top deck were directly in front of the entry/exit.
● The luggage space was tiny and not designed for buggies.
● A cord ran along the roof of the bus and was connected to a bell. Passengers or the conductor pulled it to let the driver know that he had to stop.
● A conductor, male or female, collected the money and issued the tickets from a machine that they carried.
● Conductors and drivers wore uniforms, often with collars and ties, as well as caps.
● For a long time only men could be drivers.

Talk about what it would be like to travel on a bus like this one. What were the advantages of having a conductor? Explain that a lot of people were needed to run the buses at the time when Granny was little. Discuss some of the jobs that they could have done (see 'Background information'). As London Transport didn't have enough people to work for them they recruited staff from the Caribbean.

Ask the children why people might have wanted to come to work on the buses over here. What did London Transport have to offer? Show them the recruiting poster and explain what it was offering:

● a regular job
● free uniform
● free travel on London Transport buses
● good sports facilities and canteens.

Ask the children if they think that this was a good deal. Can they think of any other reasons for people wanting to work for London Transport?

 Development

40 mins Now role-play 'The bus journey': split the children into groups of six to seven, two children to play the driver and conductor, the rest to play passengers who get on at two or three different stops. Discuss very briefly how the drivers might be feeling, what the conductor's job involves, where the passengers might be going. Allow the children a few minutes for planning, then let them role-play their imaginary journey.

After the role-play, give out copies of photocopiable page 150 and allow the children to record their thoughts.

Differentiation
Provide adult support and a pictorial vocabulary sheet for lower-ability groups.

Assessing learning outcomes
Can the children recognise two similarities and two differences between bus travel now and in the past?

Follow-up activities
● As a class, investigate other areas that recruited people who had come to Britain from the Caribbean, for example the NHS and British Rail.
● Visit a transport museum to look at old buses.
● Arrange a visit to a local bus garage.
● Invite a guest who worked on the buses as a driver or conductor to come into the school to talk to the children about their job.

① hour What was life like for those who came?

Background information
For many West Indian immigrants Britain was not an entirely unknown quantity. It was the mother country and was almost as familiar to them as their own homeland was. They learned British history in school and sang 'Rule Britannia' and 'Land of Hope and Glory'. They held British passports. However, Britain of the 1950s and 1960s was to give a huge culture shock for most of the newcomers. In the era of teddy boys, gangland conflicts and mods and rockers there was prejudice and intolerance to those who did not 'fit in'. Along with the disappointment of finding that Britain was not the place they thought it was, West Indians were met with racism and ignorance. They had to get used to different sights, sounds and expectations. They exchanged their tropical climate for one of damp and cold. Much of the food they were used to eating was unknown or difficult and expensive to obtain. Their accents and expressions were unfamiliar. Even the way they worshipped was not the same as the local church communities. Often they were met with hostility and suspicion. This applied equally to the children as well as the adults. Husbands left wives and parents left children until sufficient money had been earned in order to enable families to be reunited. Children rejoining their parents, after what may have been several years, had to re-establish relationships and get to know new brothers and sisters whom they had not yet met. Most of the Caribbean immigrants intended only to stay a few years before returning home, however many remained to make permanent homes here. They, their children and grandchildren form an integral part of our modern multicultural society. Caribbean culture has had a huge impact in some of the major cities. This is reflected in language, fashion, music, food and sport. Black Britons have contributed enthusiasm and tenacity to the culture and life of their adopted country. They are part of a trend of immigration that began with the Romans and continues today.

More information can be found on websites already mentioned in this unit and there are story books that can be used to make links, such as *Coming to England* by Floella Benjamin (Puffin Books).

Learning objective
Use sources to answer questions that go beyond simple observations to make deductions.

Lesson organisation
Pairs activity followed by whole-class discussion and then individual tasks.

What you need and preparation
Find some pictures of Britain and the Caribbean in the 1950s (you could use those collected for the first activity 'Why did people come to this country from the Caribbean?') – enough for two contrasting pictures per pair of children. You will also need: a copy of *Emerald Blue* by Ann Marie Linden (Mammoth) – optional; board or flip chart; photocopiable pages 151 and 152; writing materials.

Coming and going

Vocabulary
excitement
disappointment
surprise
joy
shock
racism
prejudice

ICT opportunities
Use tape recorders and videos to record oral history accounts. Word-process some of the transcripts.

Follow-up activities
● Gather your own oral history accounts from children and their families who have come to this area from another country.
● Hold a Caribbean celebration evening, with food and music. Invite parents in to help, to sample the children's cooking and look at displays of work.
● Look at the different cultural identities within the school and think about the benefits that they bring.
● Find out about groups or individuals who fight or fought against discrimination.

What to do

20 mins Introduction

Split the children into pairs and give each pair two pictures, one of the Caribbean and one of Britain. Ask the children what they think they would find most different when coming from the Caribbean to Britain. Encourage them to try to make specific points by referring to the pictures. Allow the children a little time to discuss their ideas. Circulate and use questions to focus those who need help, for example:

● What is the most noticeable feature of the picture?
● What impression does it give you?
● How do the pictures compare?

Now ask the whole class to listen to some of the pairs' responses. What sort of things did the children think would be most different or strange to the newcomers? Collate their answers on the board.

25 mins Development

Read some extracts from *Emerald Blue*, if you have a copy, that demonstrate what life was like in the Caribbean. Show the illustrations to the children, as these are very evocative. Explain that these are someone's memories of growing up in another place. Remind the children that they have thought about the differences that people might notice when they arrived from the Caribbean. How could we find out if these reflect what people actually experienced? Allow the children to suggest how we might find out the information.

Now read 'Sandra's story' on photocopiable pages 151 and 152, after explaining that it is a true account of a little girl who came to this country from Jamaica in the 1960s. Discuss any unknown vocabulary, then ask the children:

● Has Sandra talked about any of the things that you suggested in your earlier discussions?
● Are there any things that you take for granted that Sandra found strange when she first arrived?
● Are there any things that surprised or shocked you?

Talk about the fact that not everyone welcomed the new arrivals and that there were some people who were very unkind in the things that they said and did. What do we call this sort of behaviour? Children may well know what the term 'racism' means; some may even have experienced racist behaviour. Discuss how this makes us feel. Talk about some of the positive things that immigrants in general and those from the Caribbean in particular brought to Britain – their music, food, religion and other factors that were part of their contribution to British life.

15 mins Plenary

Ask the children record their thoughts about what Sandra found different on her arrival in Britain. See 'Differentiation' for further details.

Differentiation

Lower-ability group: with adult support discuss, and then write, one thing Sandra found unexpected about her new life. Put each person's comment in speech bubbles around a central figure of Sandra.

Middle group: storyboard three pictures of what happened to Sandra when she arrived. Write captions to accompany and explain pictures.

Upper group: write a letter (as Sandra) to Grandma back in Jamaica describing your new life. Illustrate the letter with little drawings.

Assessing learning outcomes

Can the children make deductions about Sandra's new life?

Famous events

The Programme of Study gives freedom to select just about whatever events you like from the history of Britain or the rest of the world. The examples given are *The Gunpowder Plot, The Olympic Games, other events that are commemorated*. In fact we commemorate very few events on an annual basis in this country.

The gunpowder plot is the obvious choice but it does present some problems. Of course you will want to tell the story in order to explain firework night, but any real historical study will necessitate dealing with religious intolerance and political terrorism. Children in Year 2 are capable of surprising sensitivity about such issues, but they will require careful thought. The Olympic Games are less complicated though they are not exactly 'an event'. It is important to emphasise that the present day Olympic Games are the commemoration of those that took place in Ancient Greece. The ancient games were very different, not least because they were not a contest between national teams, but between individual athletes.

Like the stories of famous people, children need to build up a stock of stories about events that will serve as milestones on their mental timelines. Where there is a timeline in the school hall or classroom, events should be added to it when they are studied. It is also recommended that the freedom allowed by the Key Stage 1 Programme of Study is used to explore events from a wide variety of times and places.

The actions of historical saints that influenced British history could be good choices, for example the landing of St Augustine, St Columba founding Iona, and the actions of St David and St Patrick. The Battle of Hastings would allow use of the Bayeux tapestry as source material. Great archaeological finds like the Chinese Terracotta Army or the ruins of Great Zimbabwe can provide good visual windows into the heritage of other cultures. Non-annual anniversaries give good excuses also – the Death of Queen Victoria in 1901, for instance.

The events chosen in this chapter are designed to provide some interesting alternatives. The priorities are to encourage maximum use of source material and to allow children to discuss the reasons for and results of past events. Events can be dealt with in a single lesson or in a mini-topic. There are three disasters (see pages 96, 98 and 99), which provide dramatic and thought-provoking stories but avoid politics and war. They will invite discussion about contemporary natural disasters around the world, with comparisons being able to be made. The story of Samuel Pepys and the Great Fire of London in 'Famous people' (see page 24) could be added to this group.

Pompeii suffered one of the most well-known volcanic eruptions of ancient times. There is a wealth of contemporary source material, including the poignant remains of the bodies themselves, of which casts have been made. The most exciting thing about the study is that the whole town was 'frozen' at one moment in time. Huge amounts of ash and pumice fell on the town and quickly covered it. The next day further inundations of ash, gas and stones followed, leaving the town buried under up to six metres of material. The depth of cover meant that no real salvage operation was possible at the time and it remained buried for 1700 years. It was rediscovered in the late 1500s, but not excavated at all until 1748. Since then digging has continued on and off, and today there are still parts of the town that have not been investigated. Pliny (see page 96) was a Roman historian and letter-writer. His uncle, a naval officer, was killed when he led a rescue attempt at Pompeii.

The sinking of the *Titanic* is well-known from the films that have been made of the disaster, but the activity in this chapter allows children to look at the story from a different perspective and is carefully based on historical fact.

The disaster at Trimdon Grange happened closer to hand. Although this took place in the north-east of England, the spectre of the mine collapse haunted all pit communities. The activity uses a folk-song as its initial source.

The mini-topic on the Moon landing allows children to celebrate some of mankind's achievements, and can also be used to encourage children to discuss the ethics of space travel.

Famous events

Enquiry questions	Learning objectives	Teaching activities	Learning outcomes	Literacy links	Cross-curricular links
What was the race for space?	• Use terms concerned with the passing of time. • Order particular events.	Investigate different 'firsts' in space exploration. Make a timeline from the results of the investigations.	Children: • order different events from the history of space exploration	Factual writing and use of information books. Use vocabulary to show the passing of time. Create a class glossary of words linked to space.	Science: identify different sources of light. Numeracy: relative sizes of planets. Design and technology: model of the Solar System.
What was special about *Apollo 11*?	• Demonstrate factual knowledge and understanding of aspects of the past and of main events and people.	Read the NASA press release. Look closely at the type of language used. What impression does it give us of that time? Show the planned sequence of events.	• identify the main facts of the proposed mission when taking notes for news reports	Look at the language of the press release that creates certain effects. Write own press release in a group and give a talk to the rest of the class.	Geography: investigate the physical geography of the moon; use images and maps of the surface.
What happened when the *Eagle* landed?	• Find answers from sources that go beyond simple observations – make deductions.	Read *The Sea of Tranquillity* to the class. Listen to a tape of the landing. Look at pictures taken on the Moon and from space. Talk about how people felt.	• make simple deductions after using a variety of sources	Write newspaper account of the event. Creative writing – poetry 'The Earth in Space'	Art: paint the Earth from Space (from photographs) and the Solar System in chalk pastels or in 3-D using papier maché. Music: listen to 'Space Oddity' by David Bowie or Holst's *Planets* suite.
Where next will we 'boldly go'?	• Give a few reasons and results of the main events and changes. • Select and combine information from sources.	Look at developments since the Apollo programme. Stress how changes have come about. Debate the future of space exploration.	• give reasons for changes and justify their points of view	Label a design for a space station or 'sky lab'.	Citizenship: consider the sustainable environment potential of space. Science: design experiments to do in zero gravity.

Enquiry questions	Learning objectives	Teaching activities	Learning outcomes	Literacy links	Cross-curricular links
What happened on Uncle Pliny's rescue mission?	● Use sources of information to gain knowledge of events beyond living memory. ● Give some reasons why people acted as they did.	Investigate volcanoes and a phenomenon. Look at what happened at Pompeii and how people tried to cope with it. Find out about the rescue attempt by Pliny's uncle.	● understand why the letter was written ● give reasons why Uncle Pliny acted as he did	Shared poetry writing; using the story as a basis for a poem describing the eruption of a volcano.	Geography: environmental issues; look at the effect of volcanoes and other natural disasters.
What was it like living in Pompeii?	● Use sources of information to gain knowledge of events in the past beyond living memory.	Use contemporary sources to investigate what life was like before the volcano erupted.	● answer questions about life in Pompeii based on the evidence from contemporary pictures	Write descriptions of what is happening in the pictures.	Design and technology: food – use Roman recipe to make bread and shape it in the same way as those in the picture of the bread seller.
What happened at Trimdon Grange?	● Find answers that go beyond simple observations to make deductions.	Investigate the mining disaster at Trimdon Grange using contemporary sources. What happened, why did it happen and what was the effect of the disaster?	● use the sources to explain what happened and why the event was a tragedy	Write a paragraph or sentence in the first person to give a viewpoint of the event. Use speech marks or speech bubbles.	Citizenship: talk about rescue services and safety issues in general. Music: look at the genre of folk-songs. Art: make charcoal pictures based on old photographs. Geography: study industry and growth and decline.
What was it like on the *Titanic*?	● Identify different ways the past is represented. ● Sequence a few events.	Discuss background information about the *Titanic*. Focus on one particular passenger and record what happened to her.	● sequence episodes from the story ● understand why two accounts of the events differ.	Use the story sheet as a Literacy Hour text and compare with other eyewitness accounts.	Music/PE: talk about how the composer evokes atmosphere; use as a basis for a dance. Art: make watercolours of the sinking to explore a restricted palette of 'watery' colours.

Moon landing

(55 mins) What was the race for space?

Learning objectives
● Use terms concerned with the passing of time
● Order events in the history of space.

Lesson organisation
Whole-class explanation; investigative group work followed by whole-class discussion; individual plenary.

Background information

The race for space began at the end of the Second World War with the German discovery of rocket science. Former German scientists were recruited to work for American and Soviet governments in developing the technology needed to escape the Earth's atmosphere. It became a visible symbol of the achievements of the two different systems of government. Each of the two superpowers was anxious to prove that they were more successful than their rival. They vied to be the first to reach space and to take control of this 'final frontier'. The greatest prize was to succeed in the race to place the first man on the moon and so to claim the new territory for the winning government.

For more information see *Journey through Space* by Tim Furniss (Hamlyn) and *The Space Atlas* by Heather Couper and Nigel Henbest (Dorling Kindersley).

Vocabulary
exploration
space
solar system
planet
astronaut
cosmonaut
Sputnik rocket
gravity
atmosphere
Soviet Union
America

What you need and preparation

You will need: a timeline on display; drawing pins or Blu-Tack; photocopiable pages 153 and 154; simple reference books on the topic of space; writing materials; scissors; glue; paper.

What to do

(10 mins) Introduction

Explain to the children that they are going to find out about different events in space travel in the mid-20th century. They will work in groups to find out some of the 'firsts' that occurred. To help them, they will have a selection of information, including a variety of images, and a photocopiable sheet to help focus their research. Either nominate a spokesperson or allow children to choose one of the group who will report back to the class with the results of the research.

Split the class into groups, directing any available adult support to the appropriate groups, and distribute the reference books and copies of photocopiable page 153.

(30 mins) Development

As the groups complete their response sheets (photocopiable page 153), circulate and help the children to structure their answers. What have they found out that is interesting? When they answer the last part of the sheet, which asks them to state what they would like to find out more about, suggest that they also form a question to which they would like to find out the answer. Give timings to the groups so that the children are aware of when they need to finish their sheets.

Call the class back together as a whole, and ask each spokesperson to report their group's findings to the rest of the class. Pin the completed response sheets onto the timeline. Points to pick up are:
● What event came first?
● How did each affect the next development?
● The Soviet Union was the first in everything except the Moon landing.

End the discussion by looking at the questions that children have identified and at the points that they found interesting. Explain why it was called the race for space and what the superpowers were trying to achieve and prove.

(15 mins) Plenary

Give out copies of photocopiable page 154 and ask the children to cut out the boxes and paste them down in sequence to form a timeline of the development of space flight.

Moon landing

Differentiation
High-ability groups can use reference information and their notes made on photocopiable page 153 as a basis for factual writing. Encourage low-ability groups to use the class timeline as a reference when they are sequencing photocopiable page 154.

Assessing learning outcomes
Can the children order different events from the history of space exploration?

ICT opportunities
Word-process labels to use with the class timeline and insert clip art as illustrations.

① What was special about *Apollo 11*?
(1 hour)

Background information
With John F Kennedy's determination that America would win the race for space and his commitment to the dream that America would be the first to land a man on the Moon, NASA had the financial backing it needed. The early disaster of AS-204 where three astronauts had been killed before take-off had occasioned some radical rethinking. Each Apollo mission got closer and closer to the goal until finally with Apollo 11 they were ready to try the ultimate test. The Moon's surface had been extensively mapped, all equipment had been tested, but there were still a lot of unknown factors and no guarantee that everything would work as expected. There were no certainties for the chosen astronauts. They were truly astronaut *explorers* as they stood ready to step into the unknown.

For more information see www.science.ksc.nasa.gov/history/apollo/apollo11.html; www.nmsi.ac.uk (Science Museum, London – key-word search *Apollo*).

Learning objective
Demonstrate factual knowledge and understanding of aspects of the past and main events and people.

Lesson organisation
Whole class for role-play; pairs activity; whole-class plenary.

What you need and preparation
Download a copy of the original press release for *Apollo 11* from NASA archives (see website address above). You will also need: a large copy of the *Apollo 11* mission badge and information about the moon shot, with some sheets on acetate or *Powerpoint* to display on screen; notebooks; writing materials; paper; photocopiable page 155. Have a copy of the first two pages of the press release recorded on audiotape for less able children.

What to do
③⓪ Introduction
(30 mins) Tell the children that they are going to take part in a role-play activity in which you will be a NASA press officer and the children will act as reporters, asking questions and taking notes. Set up the classroom as if for a news conference with some sort of podium in the front. Have the mission badge prominently displayed, perhaps on the front of the stand.

Leave the classroom momentarily then enter in role – not forgetting the obligatory American accent! Read out part of the press release, including the aim of the mission and what the astronauts will take with them. Use the OHP or *Powerpoint* to show the sequence of what the mission will attempt.

Now encourage the children to ask questions as if they were reporters. Explain that they should try to make a few notes on relevant information for a report on the proposed mission that they are going to write themselves.

Vocabulary
NASA
press release
explorer
mission
launch
lunar module
Saturn rocket

②⓪ Development
(20 mins) After the 'press conference' ask the children to split into pairs to prepare a news report. They should use their notes to write a page detailing the main points of the proposed mission. When they have finished, tell the children to practise reading their reports to each other.

Moon landing

(10) Plenary
mins Call the children together and allow some of them to read their reports to the rest of the class.

● What are the most important points that all reports identify?
● Are there any points that have not been included?

Give out copies of photocopiable page 155, one to each child, for them to complete at the end of the activity. Explain that the children should try to identify which facts are accurate.

Differentiation
Mixed-ability pairings will help less able children to write the news reports.

Assessing learning outcomes
Can the children identify the main facts of the proposed mission when they are taking notes for their news reports? The completed copies of photocopiable page 155 will allow you to assess the children's knowledge of this particular mission.

(1 hour) What happened when the *Eagle* landed?

Learning objective
Find answers from sources that go beyond simple observations – make deductions.

Lesson organisation
Whole-class discussion; individual development; whole-class plenary.

Vocabulary
lunar module
command module
landing site
Sea of Tranquillity
samples
plaque
flag
photograph
blast
descent
ascent
re-entry

Background information
On 16 July 1969, *Apollo 11* blasted off from Cape Canaveral manned by three astronauts. Its mission was to land two of the crew on the Moon, investigate the surface and then retrieve the astronauts safely before returning to Earth. The crew was made up of Neil Armstrong, Edwin 'Buzz' Aldrin and Michael Collins. Michael Collins was destined not to walk on the Moon's surface as he was to pilot the command module, *Columbia*, that would ensure the astronauts' safe return. The descent was not without drama as Neil Armstrong had to pilot the lunar module, *Eagle*, manually when it overshot the chosen landing zone. With 13 seconds of fuel to spare, the *Eagle* landed. At last, on 20 July, Neil Armstrong bravely descended the apparently frail silver ladder to the grey dusty lunar surface. It seemed that the whole world listened as he uttered those famous words: 'That's one small step for man, one giant leap for mankind.'

Later, Buzz Aldrin joined him and they filmed each other bouncing in what looked like slow motion around the spider-like lunar module. They planted a flag and left a plaque to record their momentous visit. After collecting samples of rocks and soil, they blasted back to join Michael Collins, knocking over the newly planted flag with the force of their ascent. After an uneventful return flight, they splashed down safely in the Pacific Ocean, having spectacularly secured their place in the history books and having won the space race for America.

More information can be found in *The Sea of Tranquillity* by Mark Haddon and Christian Birmingham (Picture Lions); *We interrupt this programme, 20 news stories that marked the century* by Peter Barnard (BBC Publications) – a CD-ROM with audio recordings; *The Home Planet,* ed Kevin W Kelley (Addison-Wesley) – includes stunning photography and a rich variety of eyewitness accounts.

Useful information can be found on the following websites: www.nmsi.ac.uk (Science Museum, London); www.hq.nasa.gov/osf (NASA office of Space Flight); www.hq.nasa.gov/alsj (NASA Apollo Lunar Surface Journal); www.boeing.com/news/feature/apollo11.html (provides further information on *Apollo 11*).

Moon landing

What you need and preparation

You will need: an audio recording of the event as found in *We interrupt this programme* – a video recording would also be beneficial – and playback equipment; *The Sea of Tranquillity* (see 'Background information'); images of the Earth taken from space, of astronauts, of Neil Armstrong, the lunar module and the surface of the Moon (examples of these can be obtained from the Science Museum, London); vocabulary sheets (differentiated for a range of abilities); board or flip chart; writing materials.

What to do

(30 mins) Introduction

Read *The Sea of Tranquillity* to the children. Points to bring out are:

● The excitement and sense of anticipation around the world as a whole was enormous. It was a huge adventure.

● Millions watched the event on television to see if the astronauts would succeed. The television coverage emphasised its reality.

Listen to the audio account of the actual moment of descent or watch a video recording, if you have one. Try to recreate the feeling of anticipation. If listening to the audio source, the children could listen to the commentary with their eyes closed, to aid their concentration. Ask them to try to imagine how it might have felt to have listened to this at the time. What would the general feeling have been? Give a personal account if you can remember it yourself. If possible, include a firsthand account from the astronauts (see *The Home Planet* or the 30th anniversary website.)

Encourage the children to think of how different people would have felt, such as the mission controller, Neil Armstrong himself, Buzz Aldrin waiting to go, Michael Collins in the command module, the astronauts' wives and families, the cosmonauts, the Soviet or American President, the scientists and designers at NASA, and so on. Record the children's ideas on the board.

Show the children some of the images, and encourage them to respond to them. Are there any overwhelming impressions? Does everyone feel the same? Is there anyone who feels it was a stupid or wasteful thing to do? Record any important points on the board.

(20 mins) Development

Distribute a selection of images and a vocabulary sheet or word list to each group. Ask the children to either:

● write a short account explaining why they would or would not have liked to have been Neil Armstrong, *or*

● write about the landing on the Moon from the point of view of a particular character who took part in the event.

(10 mins) Plenary

Invite the children to read out some of their accounts. What are the main features? Have they been able to justify their descriptions by explaining why they might have felt excited, frightened or upset? What sort of deductions have they made?

Differentiation

The words on the vocabulary sheets can be simplified or extended as necessary, to suit all abilities. Provide pictorial vocabulary sheets to help the least able children.

Assessing learning outcomes

Can the children make simple deductions after using a variety sources? For example *I think that it would be… because…*

CHAPTER 5
FAMOUS EVENTS

Moon landing

(1 hour) Where next will we 'boldly go'?

Learning objectives
● Give a few reasons for and results of main events and changes.
● Select and combine information from sources.

Lesson organisation
Whole-class, teacher-led discussion; class working in two halves for debate; whole-class plenary.

Vocabulary
space station
Skylab
vacuum
shuttle
environment
unmanned probes

Background information

The Apollo programme successfully landed men on the moon 17 times, thereby proving its superiority over the Soviet space programme. Gradually, however, the focus changed from competition to collaboration. This new-found spirit of co-operation was demonstrated when Soviet cosmonauts and American astronauts shook hands after successfully docking their respective crafts. The possibility of effecting a space rescue of stranded astronauts by another country was now a possibility if necessary. The superpowers now began to work more closely together. The Moon programme was wound down as the focus moved towards living and working in the vacuum of space. Exploration shifted to unmanned probes of the rest of the Solar System and beyond. The development of the space shuttle allowed astronauts better living conditions and slightly more comfortable journeys (as well as being more cost effective). Women began to take a more prominent role in the American space programme. The *Mir* space station, *Skylab* and further joint missions all pointed to the growing importance of space as an environment to be exploited for living and working in.

Further information can be found on the following websites: www.spaceflight.nasa.gov/station/index.html (International Space Station); www.lerc.nasa.gov/Doc/Search.htm; www.esa.int (European Space Agency); www.nasa.gov/women/welcomeWHM.html (women in space); www.ninety-nines.org/mercury.html (the first women to train as astronauts).

What you need and preparation

You will need: photocopiable pages 156 and 157; adult support for each group; information about the latest activities in space; images of space station, shuttle and so on; coloured counters or voting cards; writing materials.

Set the room up as a debating chamber with a central seat for the 'chair'. Give the children time before the activity to look through some reference books on space to glean useful background information.

What to do

(10 mins) Introduction

Ask the children what they think is happening now in terms of space exploration. Are they aware that NASA still exists and that the space programmes are still carrying on? You may need to point out that *Star Trek*, *Farscape* and *Star Wars* are fiction rather than reality.

Explain what has happened since the Apollo programme. Points to develop are:
● Co-operation with the Russians has led to a sharing of information and expertise.
● International missions now involve astronauts from other nations such as Japan and Britain that do not have their own space capacity.
● The space shuttle has led to larger crews, including women, and the ability to take cargoes into space as well as to have a base from which to carry out repairs to satellites, space stations and so on.
● Space shuttles are reusable and so cut costs.
● Unmanned probes have sent back stunning images and detailed information from all the planets in the solar system and some have now gone beyond, towards other stars.
● The Hubble telescope should send back clearer images of the nearer star systems.
● An international space station is being built to replace the Soviet *Mir* station. It will provide a home for astronauts to live and work in space.

- The latest target for NASA is Mars where they recently sent an unmanned probe that failed to work, much to the embarrassment of the scientists!
- NASA is working towards a manned landing on the moon within the next ten years.

Give the children a rundown of the current situation, using newspaper reports and images if possible. The NASA website has up-to-date images and information on the space station and space shuttle launches. Ask the children questions, such as Would they like to be astronauts? Would they like to land on Mars? Would they like to see the Earth from space?

Allow the children to give their responses and then explain that you are going to finish the topic with a debate about whether we should continue with the exploration of space.

ICT opportunities
Use the Internet to research further aspects of the exploration of space. Create a chart to record your investigations.

40 mins Development

Talk to the children about debates – what they are and why people hold them. Divide the class into two, each side to argue either for or against the resolution. The resolution is 'Mankind should no longer attempt the exploration of space'. Provide adult support for each half of the class and give out copies of photocopiable pages 156 and 157, which will help the children to structure their ideas.

Ask each side to appoint a spokesperson to speak for them, and explain that each side has to put forward two or three main points to support their point of view. Children from each side may ask two or three questions.

Now let the debate begin. Allow the children time to explore ideas and suggest arguments to support their viewpoint. Give support and guidance as necessary, helping the children to select main points and encouraging them to ask questions.

10 mins Plenary

At the end of the debate let each child vote on the resolution, allowing them a few minutes first to think of their response.

Give the children the result of the vote. Discuss why different people may have different points of view. Suggest that people's opinions will depend on their viewpoint – an astronaut will feel differently to a politician, for example.

If there is time, children can complete statements to show that they are aware that there may be different points of view about the same event, for example *I think people should continue to explore space because… X thinks people should not continue to explore space because…*

Finish by saying how present day advances are only possible because of developments in the past and the bravery of pioneers.

Differentiation
By outcome.

Assessing learning outcomes
Can the children use sources to justify their viewpoints?

CHAPTER 5
FAMOUS EVENTS

Pompeii

① What happened on Uncle Pliny's rescue mission?
1 hour

Learning objectives
● Use sources of information to gain knowledge of events in the past beyond living memory.
● Give some reasons why people acted as they did.

Lesson organisation
Teacher-led discussion with the whole class; individual or group work; whole-class plenary.

Vocabulary
volcano
ashes
stones
slaves

What you need and preparation
Gather together some pictures of volcanoes, and make an enlarged copy of photocopiable page 158 (or copy it onto an overhead transparency for display with an overhead projector). Find out about current disasters and rescue efforts around the world, collecting articles to show to the children in the discussion. You will also need: board or flip chart; paper; writing materials.

What to do

30 mins Introduction
Find out what the class know about volcanoes. Show them a picture of one and talk about what happens when a volcano erupts. Sometimes volcanoes remain dormant for hundreds of years before erupting, as Vesuvius did on this occasion.

Tell the children that you have a letter about a man who was killed by an erupting volcano. Read it together then bring out the following points in a discussion:
● Why was the letter written? (To help Tacitus write his book! It was actually written as source material for a history book. One of the ways that historians find out about the past is by asking people who remember it.)
● Why did Uncle Pliny take his ships into danger? (First of all, he was just curious but when he heard about the people in trouble he wanted to rescue them. You could talk about modern rescue missions to natural disasters. Talk about the courage needed to put oneself in danger to help others.)
● Which words and phrases tell us about what the volcano did? (*...a big cloud that appeared in the sky. It was shaped like a huge tree coming out of the mountain... Hot ashes were falling from the sky, then stones came crashing down... The sky was black now and stones and ash were pouring down, blocking the roads and smashing the roofs of the houses. They could see flashes of fire on the mountain.*)
● There are few aspects of the letter that place it in the Roman period but you could certainly talk about slaves and the fact that Uncle Pliny lay down for dinner, or why his friend's wife sent a slave with a letter rather than using the telephone.

20 mins Development
Work with the children to make a word web of words that describe volcanoes erupting. To help them, work through the senses, asking:
● What would you see?
● What would you hear?
● What would you smell?
● What would you feel?
Take key words and phrases from the children's responses, writing them on the board.
Now ask the children to write individual or group volcano poems, using words and phrases from the board.

10 mins Plenary
Invite several children to read their volcano poems out loud to the rest of the class.

Assessing learning outcomes
During the discussion, can the children understand why the letter was written? Can they give reasons why Uncle Pliny acted as he did?

① What was it like living in Pompeii?
hour

What you need and preparation

Collect together pictures of the remains of Pompeii. These should be very easy to find. Local libraries are likely to have books on the subject and there are a lot of images available on the Internet that children could look at in the classroom; www.tulane.edu/lester/text/western.Architect/Pompeii/ gives access to a large number of high-quality pictures. Select pictures that provide good evidence for children. Some suggestions are: the fresco of the bread seller (see website http://ps.theatre.tulane.edu), the mosaic of street musicians and the portrait of a young woman writing on a wax tablet. You could also look at www.cs.berkeley.edu/-jhauser/rome/pompeii, which has some good views of streets and the outside of shops. You will also need: board or flip chart; paper; writing materials.

What to do

⓴ Introduction
mins

Tell the children that Pompeii was a small Roman town. It stood below the volcano Mount Vesuvius near the modern city of Naples. Talk about the eruption in AD79 and how it buried the whole town. Remind the children of the story of Uncle Pliny, if you have done the previous activity. Explain how hundreds of years later, people have dug away the ash covering Pompeii and found its houses and streets. Talk about how important Pompeii is because it has helped us to find out about what it was like in Roman times. People often painted pictures of everyday life on the walls or made mosaics on the floor. These pictures show us what the people of Pompeii looked like and give us clues about their way of life.

Show a picture to the children, such as the fresco of the bread seller, and ask them:
● What is happening in the picture?
● How is it different from a modern bread shop?
● What sorts of clothes are the customers wearing?

㉚ Development
mins

Now ask the children to look at a picture of Pompeii, working in pairs or groups, and answer the following questions, which you have written on the board:
● What do you think people are doing in the picture and how do you know this?
● What are the people wearing?
● Where is this happening and why do you think this?
● What happened just before or just after this scene?
● Which of these people would you have liked to have been? (Encourage the children to explain their choices.)

⑩ Plenary
mins

Compare the children's written answers and write a selection of their key findings on the board.

Differentiation

Children who are unable to answer the questions in the development work could draw a picture of themselves dressed in similar clothes to those that the people of Pompeii are wearing.

Assessing learning outcomes

Can the children answer questions about life in Pompeii by looking at the picture?

Learning objective
Use sources of information to gain knowledge of events in the past beyond living memory.

Lesson organisation
Teacher-led discussion with the whole class; group work; whole-class plenary.

Vocabulary
Pompeii
archaeologist
evidence
fresco
mosaic
toga
tunic

Follow-up activities
● Carry out a bread-making session, copying the shapes of Roman bread, to use in an imaginary Roman bread shop.
● Focus on Roman dress, houses and cooking by looking at reference books and carrying out further activities. *Roman Food and Cooking* by Renfrew (English Heritage) contains interesting information, as well as recipes that you could try out as a class.
● Let the children take part in improvisations of life in Pompeii. Tunics and togas can be made from old sheets.

Trimdon Grange

50 mins What happened at Trimdon Grange?

Background information

In February 1882 an explosion rocked the coal mine at Trimdon Grange, near Durham. 74 men and boys were killed in the accident, leaving behind a devasted community. Almost everyone was touched by the tragedy. The prospects for the families left without the main breadwinner were bleak. Coal was the staple fuel of the 19th century, running factories and railways as well as providing the energy to heat homes and cook food. Coal-mining in the Victorian period was a very high-risk profession. Mining was labour intensive and hard physical work. Most of the coal was extracted by hand or with the judicious use of explosives. Mine galleries were dark and dangerous, often shored up merely by beams of timber. Some mines were dusty, some damp; poisonous gases were a common danger. Lighting was a constant problem and potential danger as candles could set off explosions. The Davy lamp brought some element of safety, but accidents were still common.

The Public Records Office has a wealth of sources on this disaster on its website.There is material that will allow children to reseach the tragedy using a wide range of primary sources. They will also be able to research life in the village at the time of the accident. You will find the following websites useful:

http://learningcurve.pro.gov.uk/snapshots/snapshot20.htm (Life in Trimdon Grange)
http://learningcurve.pro.gov.uk/snapshots/snapshot21.htm (Research the diaster)
http://learningcurve.pro.gov.uk/snapshots/snapshot22.htm (Song and image)

What to do and preparation

Visit the Public Records Office website and download the information that you think you will need or use. Transcribe, modify or make an audio recording of sources so that children can access the information. Make up small information packs for pairs or groups, incorporating images of mining in Victorian times. Obtain a recording of some appropriate music, if possible. The song of the tragedy was written by Tommy Armstrong. The folk-song 'Trimdon Grange Explosion' can be found on the album *Sweet Wivelsfield* by Martin Carthy on Gama Records or Lewis Killen's *Trimdon Grange Explosion*. You will also need copies of photocopiable page 159; writing materials.

What to do

20 mins Introduction

Settle the children comfortably and tell them that you want them to listen to a tale about coal-mining in the past. Read, sing or play the song 'Trimdon Grange Explosion', then question the children to draw out their understanding:

● What do they think has happened?
● Why are people sad?
● What happened to Mrs Burnett?
● What do they think exploded?
● How do they think the explosion happened?
● What did George Burnett and his brothers do?

Show the children your collected images of mining and mining rescues. Give some background to the incident and talk about what mining is and why it was so dangerous. Discuss mining in Victorian times and the types of jobs people had to do. Explain that children as well as men worked, and talk about the conditions and the hazards involved.

Now give the children the chance to offer you answers to the questions above, if they found them difficult the first time.

20 mins Development

Split the children into groups or pairs and give them a further source to investigate. (There are plenty available on the website although you may need to transcribe them or simplify them for the children's use.) Give each group or pair a character as a focus for their investigation. Explain that each of them has a piece of a jigsaw and at the end, when you have assembled all the pieces of evidence, you will be able to make a picture of what happened. Ask the children to complete photocopiable page 159, to help structure their research.

10 mins Plenary

Children report back on what they have found out. Use the information to give a picture of the event and why it happened.
● What do the children now know about the tragedy?
● Where, when and why did it happen?
● Why was it a tragedy?

Differentiation

Differentiate sources and target adult support for the less able group.

Assessing learning outcomes

Can the children use the sources to explain what happened and explain why the event was a tragedy?

Follow-up activity
Hold a class assembly in which the children present oral accounts of the coal-mining tragedy. Include a freeze-frame showing a pithead rescue scene, with children in Victorian caps, hats and shawls. Children can come 'alive' to give their version of events. Narrate the story of the explosion and give facts about Victorian mining. Finish by singing the song.

1 hour What was it like on the *Titanic*?

Background information

The *Titanic* was built in Belfast for the White Star Line. She was finished in 1912 and was the biggest ship then afloat. When she set sail on her maiden voyage on Wednesday 10 April she carried 2227 passengers and crew. She was loaded with over 5000 tons of coal. While in harbour in Southampton she used up 415 tons of coal just to keep her electrics and equipment running. Food supplies loaded included 30 000 kilos of meat and 1750 litres of ice cream. The passengers were a mixed bunch, from Lord Astor the millionaire to groups of Irish and Lebanese emigrants in the steerage.

The *Titanic* took a fairly northerly route across the Atlantic. The captain was aware of the danger from ice at that early time of year, but he was convinced that the ship was almost unsinkable. By Friday *Titanic* was running like a dream and Captain Smith was confident enough to put on speed. There was a fire in the coal store but it was not thought to be a problem.

On Sunday messages were received from other ships warning of ice ahead. Not only were these warnings ignored but the wireless operator sent a message back telling the *Californian* to 'shut up' and stop jamming his signal. At 11.40 Sunday night *Titanic* steamed straight into the ice. She scraped along the side of an iceberg and was holed in five places.

After only half an hour the decision was taken to abandon ship, but there were lifeboats for less than half of the passengers and crew. Crew members with guns attempted to reserve the places in the boats for women and children. There are stories of panic and of first-class passengers being given priority but Shaneenee's account (on photocopiable page 160) is at variance with this. Certainly none of the boats was properly filled because the people in them were so anxious to get off.

Only 705 people were saved out of the 2227. At 2.20am, the survivors in the boats saw *Titanic*'s lights go out and it sank beneath the waves. One of the last sounds heard was the band, which had kept playing to boost morale. Their last choice was 'Nearer My God to Thee'.

Learning objectives
● Identify different ways in which the past is represented.
● Sequence a few events.

Lesson organisation
Whole-class teacher-led discussion followed by paired work and whole-class plenary.

Vocabulary
Lebanon
America
cabins
passageways
lifeboats
life preserver

Titanic

Follow-up activities
● Carry out further research on the sinking of the *Titanic*.
● Develop the activity to present a dramatised class assembly.

The film *Titanic* contains many accurate and exciting episodes alongside the fictitious love story. Website www.encyclopedia-titanica.org has a great deal of source material which could be used to tell this story at any level. This lesson uses a newspaper interview given by a Lebanese woman survivor as the basis for a story of the disaster that takes a personal viewpoint.

What you need and preparation

Find sources of information about the *Titanic*, including accounts by different people. As mentioned above, the website www.encyclopedia-titanica.org has a large amount of useful information, including pictures. As well as books for adults, there are books for children, for example *Polar the Titanic Bear* by Daisy Corning Stone Spedden (Little, Brown and Company). The film is available on video and you could select parts that could be used with the story in the activity. You will also need: photocopiable page 160 (enlarged or copied onto an acetate for use with an overhead projector); board or flip chart; paper; writing and drawing materials.

What to do

ICT opportunities
Children can word-process the captions for the pictures that show the various stages of Shaneenee's timeline.

(20 mins) Introduction
Find out what the children already know about the *Titanic*. Use the background information to set the scene. You might show a clip from the video. Introduce the story as a true account of the disaster from one person's point of view. The story can be read to the children or it could be used for shared reading using an OHP. Discuss the story using key questions:
● Where was Shaneenee going?
● Where did she come from?
● Who was she with?
Discuss the children's impressions of the ship and explore which words in the story tell us about it. Encourage the children to talk about how people must have felt, referring to the story.
Now construct a timeline of the disaster from Shaneenee's point of view, sequencing episodes from the story. Choose about seven stages in her story, writing the children's suggestions for these on the board.

(30 mins) Development
Split the class into pairs, asking each pair to illustrate a different stage of the timeline. Encourage them to use source pictures for guidance, and explain that they should write a caption in their own words. Remind the children to refer to the board if they need ideas for their captions.

(10 mins) Plenary
Discuss Shaneenee's timeline by looking at the children's completed pictures and captions. Point out to the children that it is important to remember that Shaneenee saw only part of the picture and that other timelines could be constructed to show different views of events. Compare Shaneenee's timeline with one made by more able children (see below).

Differentiation

More able children can use one of the more complex accounts as a source to construct a timeline from a more general point of view. The '*Titanic* diary' on the website (see 'What you need and preparation') provides a detailed account which could be highlighted or edited for children. You can select episodes or allow the children to do so.

Assessing learning outcomes

Can the children sequence episodes from the story? Can they understand why two accounts of the events differ?

FAMOUS PEOPLE: Pioneering women
Why did Bessie Coleman go to France? Page 10

PHOTOCOPIABLE

The air show

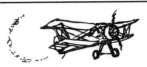 

The day was bright and sunny. Fluffy white clouds were scudding across the soft blue sky. An excited crowd was gathered in a large field. There were old and young, black and white, mothers, fathers and children. Suddenly a loud cheer went up from the waiting crowd. A small jaunty figure stepped out onto the field and waved to the expectant people gathered behind the rope barriers. She looked very trim in her khaki uniform with her Sam Browne gleaming in the sun. Her face had an infectious grin of pleasure. Bessie Coleman, the great barnstormer, was about to give one of her exciting air shows.

Bessie walked quickly towards the small biplane standing alone in the middle of the field. She climbed gracefully aboard to join her mechanic, taking the front seat. At her signal, a man came forward to start the propeller at the front of the plane. A powerful pull set the engine turning over. The little plane began to bump and bounce over the rough ground as it picked up speed. Faster and faster it raced across the field until suddenly with a lurch it rose bravely into the sky. "Hurray for Brave Bessie!" cried the crowd as the little plane climbed towards the waiting sky.

Bessie looked down at the people below who had all come to see her fly, who had all come to see her show. Now they all thought her wonderful, daring and exciting but it had been different when she had first wanted to fly. "You are black and you are a woman," she had been told. "Forget your dream, it will never happen!" Well, Bessie was stubborn and all she had had were her dreams. She had made it happen. She had saved and scrimped until she had collected enough money to go to somewhere where they would teach her, even though she was black and a woman. She had even had to learn French and had travelled, full of hope, to famous flying schools near Paris. At last, she had succeeded! Bessie Coleman, poor girl from the cotton fields of Texas, was the first black woman to earn her pilot's licence.

Expertly, she turned the controls, making the little plane swoop and dive through the air. The crowd below gasped as she climbed out onto the thin canvas covered wooden wing. She stood up, fighting against the wind as it tried to pull her from her fragile post. Her black curls escaped from her flying helmet and blew in her face. Bessie laughed into the wind. It had all been worthwhile. Soon she would have saved enough money to open her own flying school so that her people would not have to travel to France if they wanted to experience the freedom of flight. "Yes indeed," thought Bessie as she and her little plane danced through the air high above the admiring crowd, "it had all been worthwhile."

PHOTOCOPIABLE

FAMOUS PEOPLE: Pioneering women
Why was the underground railway important? Page 12

The Moses of her people

It was dark in the woods. The moon was hidden behind thick clouds and there were no stars to be seen. Harriet slipped through the trees like a ghost. In front of her stood a small rough hut. Harriet crept up to the back of the hut and began to quietly sing her special tune, "Go down Moses…" The people in the hut understood the sign and one by one they crept fearfully out. There was no talking as the little group of men, women and children followed Harriet into the night. Together they moved silently through the dark woods.

After a while Harriet stopped and felt for moss on the tree trunks to check that they were moving north. Steadily the little group followed Harriet further and further away from the plantation. With them they carried small bundles, the pitiful remnants of their lives as slaves and all they had to take into their new life. If they reached freedom safely they would have to rely on their own skills to set themselves up in this new life. As one of the smaller children began to cry with tiredness Harriet picked him up and carried him on her back. The adults plodded on, although you could have felt their fear as they jumped at the strange noises that they heard in the deep woods.

Suddenly one of the men spoke: "We can go no further, Harriet. We should go back before the plantation owners start to hunt us."

Harriet put down the child that she had been carrying and reached into the pockets of her long bulky skirt. She pulled out a pair of pistols and pointed them at the speaker. "Go free north or die," she said.

The man looked at her calm face and quickly decided to continue. All through the night the little group trekked northwards, stopping only when they had to. They needed to get as far away from the plantation as fast as they could, and reach one of the stations on the secret railway. At last, as the night was just beginning to turn to

day, they saw a house with a star quilt hung on the roof.

"That is the sign that it is safe to stay here," whispered Harriet. "These people will feed us and hide us today."

The frightened and exhausted runaway slaves stumbled towards the house. Harriet took a last look around to check that all was well, then took the hand of the smallest child, and followed the slaves into the house, relieved that they were safe.

She sells seashells on the sea-shore

Mary clambered over the rocks on the beach of Lyme Regis, hurrying towards the limestone cliffs in the distance. A little black and white dog scampered in front of her, barking excitedly. Mary's large basket banged against her side as she walked. It was empty except for her tools, the hammers and cloths and the small chisel she kept for fine work. Mary hoped that it would soon be filled with her 'curiosities'.

Mary was glad that she was able to get back to collecting her fossils again. She loved to be out searching though the rocks. She also knew how important the money they brought was to the rest of her family. Although she was only twelve, Mary was one of the breadwinners of the family.

The weather had been very bad – huge storms had battered the coast. Mary had stayed inside her little workshop helping her brother to cut and polish their curiosities. Now the sky was clear and she could venture out once more. She was looking for more of her favourite fossils, the ammonites that curled like snakes in stone, and the flower-like sea lilies or crinoids that had really been creatures not plants. She was also hoping to find more of the mysterious crocodile that she and Joseph, her brother, had been searching for. She had found some vertebrae and a strange flipper-like foot. Joseph had unearthed a huge head with a long pointed snout full of cone-shaped teeth and with enormous eye sockets. It stood now on the top shelf of the shop where Mary sold her treasures to the summer tourists. Joseph had found the head just before the great gale and Mary was sure she could find the rest.

At last Mary reached the cliffs and the high ledge where the rest of the creature might lie hidden as it had for so long. As Mary began to chip away at the rock she suddenly uncovered first one piece of backbone then another. They were too big for Mary to manage herself and she realised that she needed more help. Leaving her little dog to guard and mark the site, Mary ran to get help.

Mary and the quarrymen dug out the fossilised skeleton of the fearsome beast bit by bit. Mary's excitement grew as each part emerged. It was so large and so strange! At last they had it all and then they all helped Mary carry it back home in triumph.

Mary thought of how excited her scientist friend from the British Museum would be. It was such a strange creature, not a crocodile at all! It was like nothing that anyone had ever seen before. Mary wondered what the scientists would call it. She stroked the huge fossil and smiled.

The Maria sets sail

The covered carriages drew up at the dockside with a lurch. Once the back of the carriages were opened a group of tattered women climbed slowly out. Large, menacing men hustled them up the gangplank of the large sailing ship that was moored nearby. The women stumbled as they moved, hampered by heavy chains on their hands and feet.

The women were dirty and unkempt, their clothes were creased and some were torn. Children with tousled hair and frightened eyes clung to the women's skirts. The women were also fearful and looked around nervously. The day was grey and dull – a cold wind blew, bringing with it the sharp tang of the sea.

Another figure climbed confidently after the women. She was tall and graceful although not young. She wore a plain black cloak over her sombre grey dress, with a white scarf at her neck. On her head was a simple, white muslin bonnet. Her face was calm and kind.

Elizabeth Fry spoke quietly to the captain of the ship. She handed over a parcel of books and a purse of money. She explained to the captain that she wanted to set up a school for the children during the voyage.

"Mary here will be the teacher and I would ask thee to give her some of the money if she keeps to the task all through the journey," requested Elizabeth. Next, she and her helpers handed each of the women a bundle containing all she would need to be able to make patchwork quilts during the long voyage so that they would have something to sell once they arrived at their destination. There were even spectacles for those that needed them.

"Thou will all have time to use these before the ship docks again," she announced as she gave out the bundles. "May they be of good use to thee." Each woman also received her own comb, knife, fork and spoon. The women were overcome with gratitude and clung to Elizabeth's hand, thanking her.

"Let us pray together friends one more time and ask for God's speed on thy journey," suggested Elizabeth quietly. To the surprise of the captain and the sailors, many of whom were clinging to the rigging, the women and the children immediately knelt down on the rough wooden boards.

After praying together, the women and children were herded below deck. Elizabeth left the convict ship to wait on the quayside. The evening tide was turning and the sailors rushed to unfurl the sails. Slowly, the ship moved out of the harbour at the start of its long journey. Elizabeth sighed before turning back to her carriage. She was very tired. The women had been angry and afraid, unwilling to travel into the unknown. They had needed a lot of reassurance.

"Still, in the end," thought Elizabeth as the ship slipped beyond the distant horizon, "at least I have mananged to be of some comfort to those poor women."

FAMOUS PEOPLE: *Pioneering women*

How has medicine changed since Elizabeth Garrett Anderson became a doctor? Page 17

PHOTOCOPIABLE

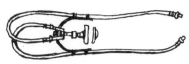 # The doctor's rounds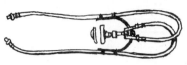

Elizabeth Garrett Anderson MD walked confidently into the ward of her latest venture, the New Hospital for Women and Children in London. She smoothed down the dark wool of her long skirt that swished importantly as she strode across the floor. She wore a smart dark jacket, with a stiff white collar and a 'bootlace tie' around her neck. Her hair was neatly tied back from her serious and determined face.

The room was light and airy with a neat row of beds on each side of the central corridor. Large arched windows above the beds let in the early spring sunshine. A coal fire in an open fireplace warmed one end of the long room. Beside some of the beds stood small tables with water jugs and china washing bowls. Not all of the beds were full although many were occupied. Most of the patients lay quietly watching the confident doctor with the kind face.

Two nurses followed the doctor. Both looked smart and businesslike with their neat white caps and aprons. They wore small metal badges to show that they were Nightingale trained nurses. Only the best was good enough for Elizabeth's hospital! All three women hurried towards the bed at the end of the ward that was hidden behind long white curtains. A woman with a badly broken leg lay in the bed. She moaned quietly as Elizabeth approached.

Elizabeth laid a cool hand against the woman's hot head.

"We must operate, Mary Anne, or you will never again walk without a limp," she gently told the waiting woman.

"No, no," groaned Mary Anne, " I'll die under the knife or lose the leg. I cannot stand the pain. How will my family manage if I am a cripple," she cried fearfully.

"Doctor Garrett Anderson is one of the best doctors there is. You will be safe in her hands," said the staff nurse reassuringly.

"We will use the new anaesthetics," explained Elizabeth. "You will fall asleep and when you wake up again it will be all over. You will be safe, Mary Anne, and you will walk again," she assured the terrified woman.

Mary Anne closed her eyes as the doctor's calm voice soothed her fears. Shortly, two strong porters came to take her to theatre.

Elizabeth hurried off to get ready for the operation. Then she looked around with quiet contentment as she walked into her well-organised theatre and remembered those long years of study and how everyone had told her that she couldn't do it, that women couldn't be doctors.

PHOTOCOPIABLE

FAMOUS PEOPLE: *Pioneering women*
How has medicine changed since Elizabeth Garrett Anderson became a doctor? Page 17

Name _____ Date _____

Medicine now and in Victorian times

Look at the two pictures. They show the sort of hospital ward that Elizabeth Garrett Anderson would have known and the sort that you would see today.

A ward in Elizabeth Garrett Anderson's time

A ward today

Find two things that are the same now as in Victorian times.

_____ _____

Find something that is found in hospitals today that was not found in Victorian hospitals.

_____

Find something that was found in Victorian hospitals that is not found in hospitals today.

_____

Leonardo da Vinci

Piero lived in the country near Florence in Italy, over five hundred years ago. He was walking one day when he saw a farmer friend of his. "What are you up to?" he asked.

"I have just cut down this tree and I was thinking what to make with the wood," answered his friend. "I think I shall make a shield so that when I go travelling I can protect myself against thieves with swords."

"When you've made it, I will get my son to paint something on it for you," said Piero.

Piero's son Leonardo had just become an apprentice to a famous painter called Andrea del Verocchio who painted pictures to hang in the churches in Florence. Leonardo was a clever boy and he seemed to be good at everything he tried. His trouble was the fact that he started so many things that he often did not get round to finishing them. He loved having a new problem to solve and he was delighted when his dad brought the shield for him to paint.

"What shall I paint?" he wondered. "It should be something really scary to frighten off the thieves if they just look at it." He thought and thought of all the things he might put on the shield, but he kept changing his mind and finding other interesting things to do. By the time he got around to starting it, his dad had forgotten all about it.

Leonardo started to make a collection. He loved animals. If he saw a bird in a cage in the market he used to buy it just to let it go free, but this time he looked down drains and under stones and in the attic, and gathered all the scary things he could find. He had a lizard, a snake, some big hairy spiders, a dead rat and lots of other slimy, slithering, smelly, spiky creatures. He hid them all in his bedroom. Before he painted anything he looked hard at each creature and drew it very carefully. Then he started to paint a monster on the shield. It had lizard legs, eight spider arms, a ratty face and a forked snake tongue, and a few other nasty bits as well. When he had finished it looked brilliant. He covered up the window and made the room dark, then he shone a candle on the monster, and he waited for his dad to visit.

Poor Piero walked up the stairs and opened the door. Then he nearly jumped out of his skin. Before him in the darkened room he could see only this horrible thing. Leonardo had painted it so well that it seemed to be alive and the monster seemed to be moving in the flickering candlelight. When he recovered, Piero realised that his son was very special; he had never seen a picture as lifelike as the monster before and he did not think anyone but Leonardo could have done it.

Leonardo became one of the greatest painters ever. (You can still see lots of his pictures today.) But he never stopped being interested in just about everything. He made drawings of his ideas for making a helicopter and a parachute hundreds of years before anyone else thought of such things, but he never got around to making them. He did design buildings, make jewellery, write poetry and play musical instruments, and he did all these things well. Best of all, he was kind and gentle and liked a joke.

PHOTOCOPIABLE

Francis Drake and the voyage of *The Golden Hinde*

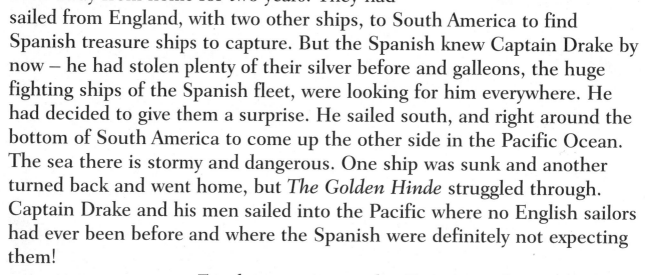

"We want to go home, Captain, and we are going the wrong way," shouted the big sailor in the woolly hat. There were about fifty sailors standing in a crowd, barefoot on the deck of the ship. The ship heaved up and down on the sea, and the great white sails blew out like sheets on a washing line. The ropes squeaked and the wooden ship creaked while seagulls squawked in the windy sky.

The ship was called *The Golden Hinde* and the captain was Francis Drake. He and his men had been away from home for two years. They had sailed from England, with two other ships, to South America to find Spanish treasure ships to capture. But the Spanish knew Captain Drake by now – he had stolen plenty of their silver before and galleons, the huge fighting ships of the Spanish fleet, were looking for him everywhere. He had decided to give them a surprise. He sailed south, and right around the bottom of South America to come up the other side in the Pacific Ocean. The sea there is stormy and dangerous. One ship was sunk and another turned back and went home, but *The Golden Hinde* struggled through. Captain Drake and his men sailed into the Pacific where no English sailors had ever been before and where the Spanish were definitely not expecting them!

For the next six months, Francis Drake and his men raided towns and captured ships. The Spanish were so surprised to see him that they usually gave up without fighting. Drake took their silver and freed their slaves and then was off again before they really knew what was happening.

But then the Spanish grew tired of the attacks and decided to take action. They sent out a fleet of galleons to capture him. *The Golden Hinde* was all alone and so full of silver that it moved rather slowly.

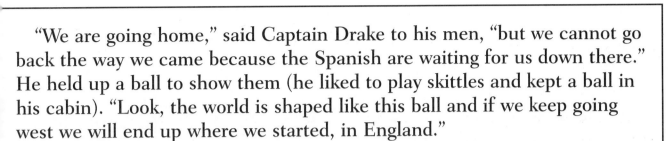

"We are going home," said Captain Drake to his men, "but we cannot go back the way we came because the Spanish are waiting for us down there." He held up a ball to show them (he liked to play skittles and kept a ball in his cabin). "Look, the world is shaped like this ball and if we keep going west we will end up where we started, in England."

"Don't be stupid," roared the big sailor. "How can the world be shaped like a ball? We would all fall off it. Everyone can see that it is flat."

"I don't quite understand it myself," answered Drake calmly, "but I know that a Portuguese ship went right around the world fifty years ago and ended up where it started. If they can do it then so can we."

The men were not at all sure about this, but they all trusted Francis Drake, and *The Golden Hinde* sailed west away from the Spanish fleet into the unknown. Drake had no maps to help him and there was no TV or radio or telephones or any way of contacting anyone. He used a compass to make sure he was heading west and watching the stars at night helped him tell the right direction. He stopped at various islands on the way and met all sorts of people but none of them spoke English or could tell him the way home. He used signs to talk to them and usually made friends and swapped some of his treasure for food and drink. There were storms and accidents and once they got stuck on a sandbank near India for days, but one autumn day, over a year later, the lookout sighted England.

The Golden Hinde sailed up the Thames to Deptford, loaded with treasure – the first English ship to sail around the world and the second ship ever to do so. Queen Elizabeth came down to meet the ship (and get her share of the treasure). She made Captain Drake a knight so then he was known as Sir Francis Drake. He went home to Devon and bought himself a nice house in the country, which you can go and see if you go there on holiday. He spent some of his treasure digging a canal to bring clean water to his hometown of Plymouth, but he soon went back to sea.

FAMOUS PEOPLE: Men of their time
Who was Francis Drake? Page 23

Arguments

We must go home the way we came.	If we go back the way we came the Spanish will catch us.
The world is flat.	The world is like a ball. If we go on we will end up where we started.
We have got enough treasure now and I want to go home quickly.	It will be exciting to see new places.

FAMOUS PEOPLE: **Men of their time**
Who was Samuel Pepys? Page 24

PHOTOCOPIABLE

Samuel Pepys and the Great Fire of London

Samuel Pepys was woken up in the middle of a loud snore by his maid Jane calling from the door. "Wake up, master, there is a fire in the city!"

His wife stuck her head out from under the covers: "What is it, dear?"

"I will go and see," said Samuel Pepys. He got up and pulled on his dressing gown over his long night-shirt. It was the middle of the night and Jane held up a candle to help him find his way to the window. The night was dark but across the rooftops he could see an orange glow in the sky and yellow flames flickering around a burning house. He watched for a while but he was getting cold standing there and the fire seemed a long way away so he went back to bed and slept.

When he woke up again in the early morning he found that Jane had been out already to find out the news. Three hundred houses had been burned down and the fire was getting bigger and bigger. He got dressed and went out. The houses in London were mostly made of wood then and many roofs were thatched with straw, so they caught fire easily. Samuel Pepys walked to the Tower of London and climbed up on a high wall to see better. Everywhere houses were burning and people were running about trying to save some of their belongings before their houses were destroyed. The wind was blowing the flames from one house to the next and the fire was moving steadily along. Everyone was heading for the river and some were climbing into boats to escape. He saw that even the pigeons on the

roofs were in a panic. Some of them flew too close to the flames and fell out of the sky.

Pepys worked for the King and he hurried to Whitehall to tell him about the terrible fire. A crowd of people were with the King, discussing what to do. There were no fire engines then, only buckets to carry water from the river and long hooks to pull down the burning thatch, but the fire was too hot

PHOTOCOPIABLE

FAMOUS PEOPLE: Men of their time
Who was Samuel Pepys? Page 24

and dangerous now to get near it. The only thing to do was to pull down the houses in the path of the fire so that it would run out of things to burn and die down by itself. The King sent Pepys to find the Lord Mayor of London and tell him what to do. He found him rushing down the street with a wet handkerchief around his face and gave him the message. "What can I do?" said the mayor. "I am exhausted, the people will not obey me, I have been pulling down houses but the fire keeps catching up with us before we have finished."

The fire raged and burned. St Paul's Cathedral was destroyed. The fire was so hot that the stones cracked and flew like bombs and metal gutters melted. The pavements glowed red so you could not walk on them. Thousands of people were driven out by the flames and camped in the fields around London in tents made from blankets or sheets. Churches and great buildings crashed to the ground and at night the sky was as bright as day from the light of ten thousand houses burning.

In the end, the King got sailors from his ships to blow up houses with gunpowder to try and stop the fire. After three days the wind eased and at last the fire died down with it.

Samuel Pepys was lucky that his house was saved, and he went home to sleep. The next day he got out his diary and wrote down all he could remember of those awful days. He wrote his diary in a secret code so no one else could read it, but two hundred years later someone found it and worked out his code.

Now The Diary of Samuel Pepys *is a very famous book. It is special because when we read it we can find out what happened from someone who actually saw it all. Another man, called John Evelyn, also saw the fire and wrote about it in his diary. You can look at his account too.*

FAMOUS PEOPLE: **Men of their time**
Who was Samuel Pepys? Page 23

PHOTOCOPIABLE

What's the order?

He hurried to Whitehall to tell the King about the fire.

The next day Pepys got out his diary and wrote down all he could remember.

In the end the King got sailors to blow up the houses with gunpowder.

In the morning Samuel Pepys climbed up on a high wall to see better.

"Wake up, master, there is a fire in the city!"

The Lord Mayor said, "What can I do? The people will not obey me."

PHOTOCOPIABLE

FAMOUS PEOPLE: **Men of their time**
Who was William Hogarth? Page 25

William Hogarth's London

The elegant Mr David Garrick, the famous actor, strolled along arm in arm with his friend, William Hogarth. Garrick was dressed in a beautiful blue coat with gold buttons; his walking cane was also topped with a golden ball. White lace spilled out from his cuffs and collar and his wig was dusted with white powder. Hogarth was short and square with a rusty brown coat and a short, square, brown dog trotted beside him.

The streets of London were crowded and noisy. "Make way!" came a shout, as two men jogged by with a sedan chair. Mud splashed up as they passed, and sprayed a girl selling shrimps from a basket. She yelled names after them but her voice was drowned by the sound of hautboy and drum as two street musicians came around the corner. A window was flung open in the nearest house and an angry head poked out, "Stop that racket, I'm trying to work in here!" A little girl swung her rattle in the air to add to the pandemonium and with a crash a workman emptied out a load of stones to mend the pavement.

"What a place to live," said Garrick covering his ears.

"What a place," agreed Hogarth as he took out a pencil and scribbled a tiny sketch on his own thumbnail.

A few minutes later, the two men were sitting in their favourite haunt, The Bedford Coffee House. Garrick called for two bowls of hot chocolate, and Hogarth called for a sheet of paper. "Here we go again," said Garrick. "Can't we go for a drink without you working on your next picture?"

Hogarth smiled but he was too busy drawing to answer.

Hogarth was always looking around him, at the interesting faces of the people in the street, at the funny things and the sad things happening around him. He remembered it all and made little sketches on his nails or on odd bits of paper. In his studio he turned the sketches into pictures. There were no

films or videos then, but his pictures are a bit like videos. Nothing in the pictures is standing still and you can practically hear the noise and smell the smells of London. They tell stories too. If you look carefully you can guess what is happening and what the characters are saying.

When he finished a picture, Hogarth took out a small sheet of copper. He spent nearly an hour polishing it, first with stone then with charcoal and last with stale bread. In the end it shone like a mirror. He took his burin, a sharp tool, and began to scratch a copy of the picture onto the copper. Wherever there was white paper showing on the picture he cut down into the copper. Where there was a black line he left the surface alone. He wrote the title underneath, but he wrote it backwards. In the end he dabbed the plate with ink and laid a piece of paper on top, then pressed over it with a wooden roller. When he took the sheet of paper off, there was a copy of his picture printed on it (and the writing came out the right way around).

He gave the plate to the printer and he would make hundreds of copies of the picture. People came from all over London to buy the latest Hogarth print when it came out. Everyone liked them – rich people and poor, clever people and not so clever – because they recognised the characters. They laughed at the way he made them look funny, but there was a serious side too. He often showed up the silly or cruel things that went on around him.

If you want to know what London was like in the 18th century you only have to look at William Hogarth's pictures. There is always something new in them if you look carefully.

FAMOUS PEOPLE: Men of their time
Who was Isambard Kingdom Brunel? Page 27

PHOTOCOPIABLE

Isambard Kingdom Brunel and the GWR

There was a clattering of horses' hooves and a rumble of wheels outside the office and Isambard jumped up from his stool in front of the drawing board. "Come on Joseph, I want you to look at what I have bought." Isambard Kingdom Brunel was very short, but tough looking – he always moved very fast and expected everybody else to as well. He was an engineer who could design and build just about anything. Joseph Bennet was in charge of Isambard's office.

In the street outside was the new 'britschka'. "What on earth is a britschka?" enquired Joseph.

Isambard showed him. It was a big cart pulled by four horses, but inside it, was a bed, a drawing board and cupboards for everything. "This one is for my pencils and rubbers and rulers and other designing equipment. Down here I will keep my compass and theodolite and the stuff for surveying. Look at this little paraffin stove for making my coffee, and the pot and cups. See the bookcase has a bar across it to stop the books falling out."

"Are you intending to live in it?" laughed Joseph.

"I may have to," said Isambard quite seriously. "A lot of people sneered when I called our company the Great Western Railway, but it is going to be the best railway in the world. I want everybody to be able to travel fast while drinking coffee and reading a book, just like me in the britschka.

Railways had only been invented for a short while and people had to

walk or travel on horseback or in a stagecoach, which was very bumpy and uncomfortable. The roads were mostly muddy and full of big holes. Brunel planned to build a railway line from Bristol to London over 190 kilometres. He had to look carefully at maps and choose the best route. Trains are not good at going up hills so he had to find a reasonably flat path for

FAMOUS PEOPLE: Men of their time
Who was Isambard Kingdom Brunel? Page 27

PHOTOCOPIABLE

the rails. Then he had to drive in his britschka along every kilometre of the way finding out who owned each bit of land and persuading them to let him build his railway over it. Often he drove frantically up and down the country all day, talked and argued with the landowners all evening and sat up half the night writing important letters to the office. Then he had to carefully measure and work out how high the hills were and draw his own maps of the route. Where he could not avoid a steep hill he made plans to dig a tunnel through it. As he moved about he had ideas about what sort of rails to use and how he would design the carriages.

At last the plans were complete and the day came when Brunel had to go to parliament to get permission to build the railway. A lot of rich men did not want him to get it and they were determined to catch him out and show that he had made mistakes. For eleven days they questioned him on just about every detail of his designs. They asked him exactly how long each tunnel was, and how much earth needed to be moved to build it. They grilled him about how high the land was at each point and how the bridges would be built over the rivers on the way. They even asked a lot of stupid questions but Brunel stayed cool and knew all the answers. He got permission to build his railway.

For the next six years Brunel did not stop and he lived about half the time in the britschka driving up and down the land between London and Bristol drawing, designing, arguing with landowners and supervising the hundreds of workers building the line. He built bridges and viaducts and dug tunnels and cuttings. He built great stations like Paddington and even spent time on designing the badge to go on his engines.

The Great Western Railway was the best, fastest, most comfortable railway in the world for many years. Brunel built lots of other things as well that you can still see today because he understood design and technology so well and always checked every single detail.

FAMOUS PEOPLE: *Men of their time*
Who was Isambard Kingdom Brunel? Page 27

PHOTOCOPIABLE

A good thing or a bad thing?

The railway will be noisy.

We will be able to get to London in a few hours instead of two days.

The smoke will pollute the atmosphere.

It will not matter about the weather.

People were not meant to fly about at that speed.

We will be able to eat and drink while we travel.

It will put the stagecoaches out of business.

The stagecoaches are bumpy and out of date.

It's all right but not near my home.

There will be more things in the shops because we can send goods by rail.

FAMOUS PEOPLE: Men of their time
Who is Nelson Mandela? Page 28

PHOTOCOPIABLE

Nelson Mandela and the Rugby World Cup

South Africa is a big country and millions of people live there. Some of the people are white and speak English or Afrikaans, there are people whose families came from India who speak Gujerati or Punjabi, but most people are black and speak Xhosa or Zulu. There are many languages spoken in South Africa and all sorts of people. Sometimes it is called 'the Rainbow Nation'.

For many years the white people in South Africa were in charge of everything. The black people could not even live where they wanted to and it was very hard for them to go to college or university and get a good education.

Nelson Mandela was a boy from the country who worked very hard at school and went to university. He became a lawyer and he and his friend Oliver Tambo were the first black men to set up a law firm in South Africa. They especially helped poor black people who were being moved from their homes because the land had been given to white people. Mandela was soon in trouble with the police himself because he argued that everyone in South Africa should be equal and that there should not be one law for white people and another for black people.

Mandela was put in prison and it was very hard. He was given poor food and had to break up big stones with a hammer all day. He was kept in prison for twenty-eight years.

While he was in prison, things in South Africa got worse and worse. People became angrier and angrier with one another. The black people wanted to be treated the same as white people but the government would not listen to them. There was fighting and people were hurt and killed. It looked as though there was no way to make peace.

President De Klerk sent for Nelson Mandela. The two men realised that they had to find a way to be friends. De Klerk was the head of the white government that had put Nelson Mandela in prison for twenty-eight years. Some of Mandela's friends told him not to talk to De Klerk because he was his enemy, but he went anyway. It took a lot of difficult talking but at last it was agreed that there would be an election in South Africa and everyone, black and white, could vote for a new government. There was great excitement as millions of people queued up for hours to take their turn putting a cross on a piece of paper to choose the new leaders. When the votes were counted up it became clear that Nelson Mandela was to be the new President of South Africa.

Soon after the election the Rugby World Cup was held in South Africa. The South African team, the Springboks, won their matches and when it came to the final they had to play against the New Zealand team. In South Africa, rugby was generally a white person's game while black people mostly played football so no one expected Mandela to be interested. When the teams ran out onto the pitch there was a black man running in front of the Springboks. It was Nelson Mandela, President of South Africa, wearing a rugby shirt. Nelson Mandela stood proudly and sang two songs. He wanted everyone to forget the past and share in the new 'Rainbow nation'.

Name _____ Date _____

Holiday questionnaire

What do you remember about your holidays as a child?

-
-
-

Where did you go? (UK/abroad/country/seaside)

Who went with you?	How long did you go for?

When did you take your main holiday?

How did you travel there?

What was your favourite holiday, when did you take it and why do you remember it so well?

Name _____   Date _____

Holidays worksheet

Describe two things that are the same about holidays now and in the past.

_____

_____

Describe two things that are different about holidays now and in the past.

_____

_____

Complete this sentence:

People go on holiday because _____

_____

Draw a picture of a holiday scene, either now or in the past.

PHOTOCOPIABLE

THEMATIC STUDIES: The seaside at the turn of the century
What were holidays like long ago and who went on them? Page 34

Rosie's day at the seaside

Rosie opened one eye and lifted her head from the pillow very gently. She slept in the middle between her two big sisters, Laura and Eve, and they would be grumpy if she woke them up by wriggling too much. Through the iron bars of the bed she could see the thick dark curtains of the window and, sure enough, there was bright sunlight showing around the edge. At last it was morning, and a very special morning at that. The door opened and Pa's head peered round it. "Come on girls, all those coming to the seaside, hair brushed, dressed and on parade in half an hour."

What with washing and dressing and breakfast and Mother remembering things she had forgotten and Pa going back to make sure the kitchen fire was safe, it was two hours later before the family rolled up at the station in a 'growler'. This was another treat as Rosie had never been in a cab before. It was great fun rattling along even though she had to sit on brother Jack's knee with one end of the huge picnic hamper on top of her and mother's parasol poking her on the nose every time the cab went

over a bump. People stopped and stared as they arrived at the station and all piled out. There was Pa pulling one end of the hamper with Jack at the other (Jack was grown up and went to work with Pa on the railway). Next came Mother with her parasol, and her carpet bag (which contained important things like spare stockings and knickers for the girls, smelling salts and liver pills, rags for mopping up messes, and towels for bathing). Then came Laura carrying Len. Eve and Rosie came last, each with a parcel containing their bathing suits. The poor horse that had pulled them all to the station looked ready to collapse.

Inside the huge station the family had to hang on to one another to stay together in the great, jostling, bustling, hurrying crowd. The air smelled of smoke and steam, and deafening screeches and clangs and honks came from the engines as they crawled in or out of the platforms.

Because Pa and Jack were railwaymen they did not have to buy tickets. They showed their free pass as the family marched proudly past the barrier. "Morning Bill,

THEMATIC STUDIES: **The seaside at the turn of the century**

What were holidays like long ago and who went on them? Page 34

PHOTOCOPIABLE

morning young Jack, morning missis," said the ticket collector.

"We're going to the seaside," said Rosie.

"You mind you don't get swallowed by a whale," said the ticket collector. Rosie thought he was probably joking so she laughed.

The train was a great long one and they had to make sure they did not get into the carriages with a 1 on the door or a 2 on the door because they were for rich people. Unfortunately, everyone seemed to be getting into the carriages with a 3 on the door and it was rather a squash.

Eventually they managed to get a compartment with only two other people in it, an old lady and a grown-up girl, so Mother and Pa and Jack and Laura could sit down with Rosie, Eve and Len on laps. The journey was magical. They all got more and more excited until Pa said, "Not another word till you see the sea, and the first one to spot it gets a mint humbug."

Of course they all saw the sea together so Pa had to buy them all mint humbugs. Outside the seaside station the wonderful salty breeze smelled quite different from the smoky city, and down the hill, past the little town, Rosie saw the sea. It went on for ever, sparkling in the sunshine under a big blue sky with no big buildings to block the view. Rosie thought that she would explode with excitement before the family and its luggage at last struggled down the steps from the promenade onto the crunching shingle of the beach.

There were lots of families on the beach already but they found a spot to spread out the big blanket and Mother sat down next to the hamper with the parasol propped up to shade her. Mother was having another baby soon and she said that she was getting too big to run about much on the sand. Pa and Jack took off their jackets and rolled up their sleeves. Pa even took off his cloth cap and put a knotted handkerchief on his head.

The children took turns to hold up the towels while they undressed and put on their bathing suits. Laura had a proper one that was only a few years old and had belonged to Auntie Em; Eve and Rosie had knitted ones that Mother had made. Rosie's had stripes – the brown stripes were wool from Pa's old pullover and the beige ones were

an old muffler of Jack's. But as soon as they were ready, the clouds started to roll in and it wasn't long before they had to change back into their clothes. Mother didn't want them to get a chill.

Pa took the young ones up to the kiosk on the prom and they chose two lovely little buckets with fish painted on them and two little wooden spades. Len got a paper windmill on a stick that spun around really fast if you ran with it. Eve took it from him to show him how to use it, but she took a very long time showing him all the different ways and he cried and Pa made her give it back.

They paddled in the sea, and tried to race the waves back in – they couldn't believe how icy cold the water felt. It was freezing! Then they made a big sandcastle together and Pa helped with his boots off and his trouser legs rolled up to his knees. Mother had remembered to bring crayons and some paper so they made a flag for the castle and used a lolly stick as a flag-pole.

At lunchtime they had scrambled egg sandwiches, and sardine sandwiches and fish paste. They had Rich Tea biscuits for afters. They had bottles of water to drink, but afterwards Pa and Jack went to have a beer and Jack brought down bottles of fizzy lemonade from the pub as his treat.

When the men came back, Pa said that he had seen a poster and that there was to be a Punch and Judy show on the other side of the pier in an hour. So they packed everything up. The men had met the old lady from the train further along the beach and she said she would look after the hamper and bags to give Mother a chance to look about a bit. It was a bit frightening on the end of the pier when you were right over the top of the sea and you could see it washing around through the planks.

The Punch and Judy was a great success. At three o'clock it was time to go back to the station and everyone was a bit tired and grumbly. But it was a wonderful day!

THEMATIC STUDIES: The seaside at the turn of the century
What did people do at the seaside long ago? Page 37

PHOTOCOPIABLE

Worthing
'A dip in the briny'

Bathing in Worthing is perfectly safe due to the gently sloping beach. Bathing machines can be reserved at a cost of 9d per half-hour, or 1s for ladies who require an attendant to help them dress. There are also dressing tents at each end of the town. Gentlemen and boys over seven years of age may use the West end of the beach and ladies the East. There is now also an area for mixed bathing beside the pier. Gentlemen may also swim from boats at the pier head in the morning.

For those who enjoy fishing and boating, boats can be hired for 2s per hour with a boatman or 1/6 without. Sailing boats can be had for 4s for up to ten people.

The bandstand is occupied by a high-class military band that gives weekly promenade concerts in Steyne Gardens. Other attractions such as minstrel shows and the popular 'Punch & Judy' may be regularly seen around the pier. Donkey rides are a favourite with the children and those for hire on the sea front are regularly inspected.

Paddle steamers leave daily from the pier head for Brighton, and other excursions to the countryside are possible through Worthing's modern motor omnibus service.

The London, Brighton and South Coast Railway provide regular trains to Worthing, fast trains taking only one hour and a quarter for the journey.

Fares:	1st Class	2nd Class	3rd Class
London Bridge	15/4	10/6	9/2
Victoria	15/4	10/6	9/2
Clapham Junction	15/1	10/6	8/4

Name _____   Date _____

Seaside resort

These people are on the beach 100 years ago.

What are they watching?

What are they wearing?

What do you wear on the beach?

The park at the turn of the century

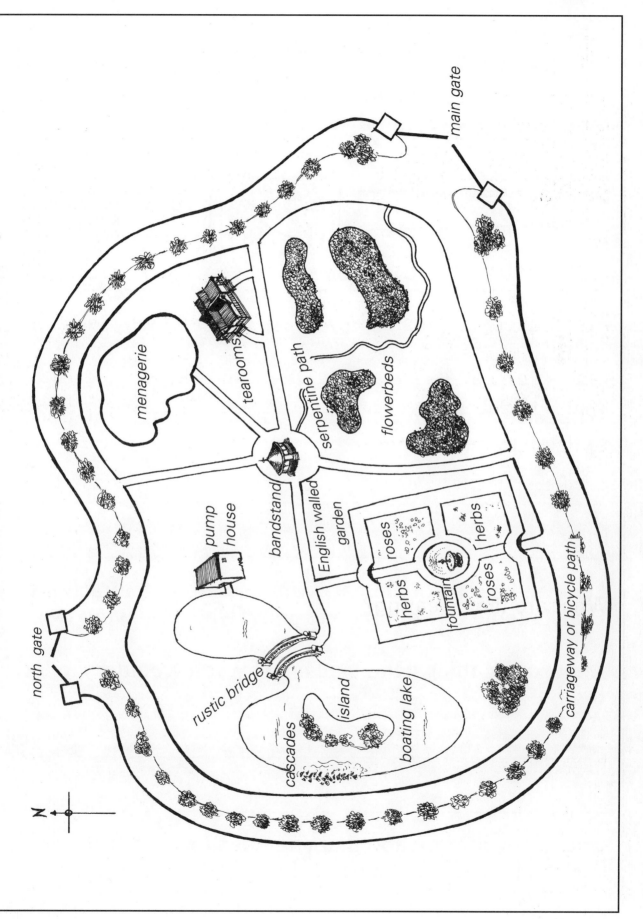

main gate

menagerie

tearooms

serpentine path

flowerbeds

English walled garden

roses

herbs

herbs

roses

fountain

pump house

bandstand

north gate

rustic bridge

cascades

island

boating lake

carriageway or bicycle path

N

Name _____ Date _____

 Entertainment

Look at the pictures and books about the music halls. Draw a picture showing some of the sights that you might have seen. Use the books to help you.

Listen to the band music. Write down three words that describe how you feel.

_____

Which piece of music did you like best and why was this?

_____

What else might you do with your afternoon if you don't go to listen to the band?

_____

_____

Look at the map of the park with its different attractions. Draw a route on your map to show what you would visit.

Choose two things and explain why you would go to look at them.

_____

_____

Staple any information that you have found out about Punch and Judy to the back of this sheet.

Name _____   Date _____

Bread research sheet

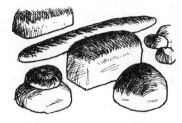

What period are you researching?

_____

What type of bread did poor people eat in this period?

_____

What type of bread did rich people eat in this period?

_____

Where did people make their bread at this time?

_____

Did people have any special names or words associated with bread at this time?

_____

_____

Can you draw a picture to show people making or eating bread at this time? Use a separate sheet of paper.

Find and copy out a bread recipe for this period on another sheet of paper.

The history of bread

Cut out the sections and match them together under the correct period.

Ancient Egyptians	Romans	Victorians	Tudors	Medieval period	2000s
Many modern supermarkets bake bread in the store and have different types of bread from all around the world.	Poor people ate brown bread with rye barley or even peas or beans added to it to make it cheaper.	Hot bread rolls in fancy shapes, scones, cakes and pastries with home-made jams and preserves made teatime important for rich Victorians.	In a medieval castle people baked flat loaves to use instead of plates.	These people ate flavoured bread dipped in wine or goat's milk. Roman loaves were often round with notches cut into them.	Here are some hieroglyphs that were found from Ancient Egyptian times and that mean bread.

PRIMARY FOUNDATIONS: History Ages 5–7

Baking in the past

PHOTOCOPIABLE

Name _____   Date _____

Baking in the past

Look at your picture. What can you see happening? Write down or draw three things that you think are important.

Would you have liked to be this baker? Why do you think this?

Were bakers important people? Why do you think this?

Map for your castle

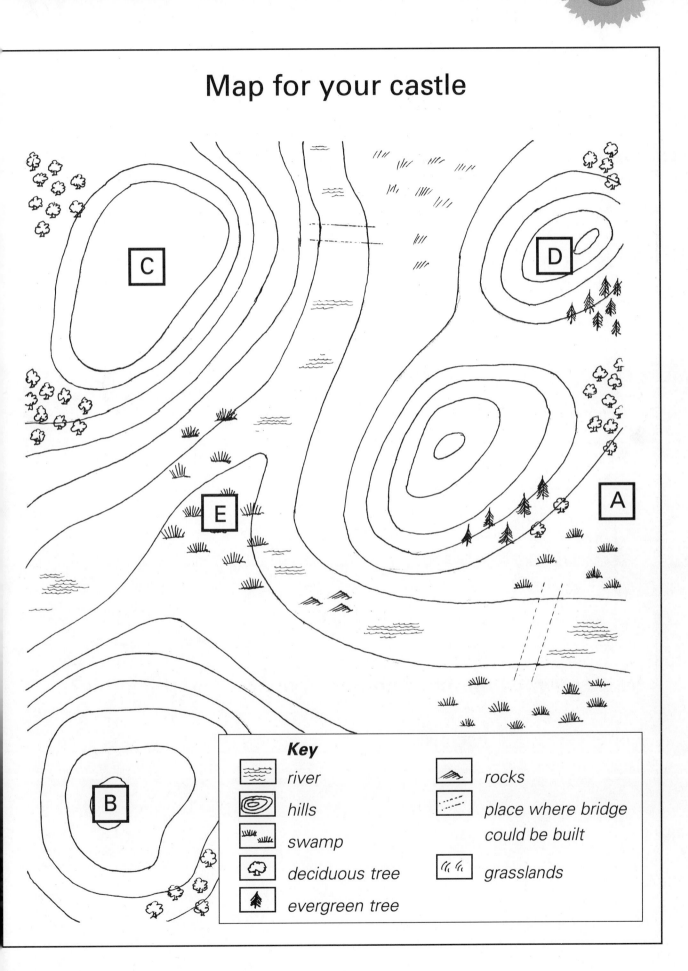

Key

~	river	rocks	rocks

- river
- hills
- swamp
- deciduous tree
- evergreen tree
- rocks
- place where bridge could be built
- grasslands

Name _____ Date _____

Building the castle

The king has given you the land shown on the map. Decide on which of the sites to build your castle. Use the table to help you to come to a decision.

	Good visibility	Height	Water	Track/ road	Fuel source	Level ground
Site A						
Site B						
Site C						
Site D						
Site E						

Key
*** very easily available
** available
* not easily available
o not available at all

Now say why you have chosen that site.

I chose Site ___ because

Name _____   Date _____

Castle plans

Look at the ground plan below which shows how a castle might be organised.
Think about the different areas that you can see.

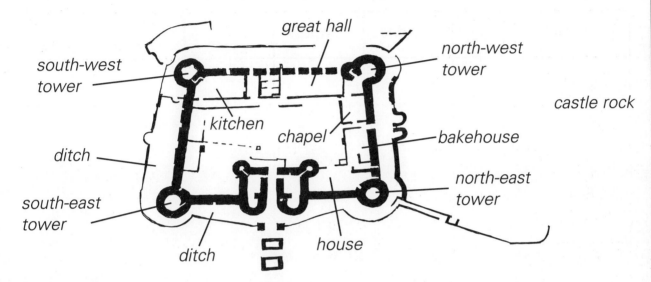

Try to decide what the different parts were used for.
● Colour red the parts that were used for defence.
● Colour blue the parts that people lived in.

Each castle was different as this made them more difficult to attack.
On your large piece of paper decide, as a group, the sort of castle you would build. Label the different parts. You can use the following words to help you decide what to include.

moat or ditch	tower
keep	stable
drawbridge	barbican
great hall	bakehouse
battlements	gatehouse
chapel	courtyard

Is there anything else that you think you would need to include?

Name _____   Date _____

Who worked in the castle?

Think of three or four things to describe yourself. You may want to think about whether you are a man or woman, old or young, whether you have been educated or if you have to be very fit to do your job.

What is your job called?

What sort of things do you have to do?

What part of the castle do you work in?

Do you like or dislike you job and why?

What would you like to change about your job?

Complete the sentence
My job in the castle is important because

Draw a picture of yourself at work
on a separate sheet of paper.

PERIODS BEYOND LIVING MEMORY: Castles in the Middle Ages
What was life like for the children of the lord? Page 56
PHOTOCOPIABLE

The contrast between rich and poor

	The lord's only daughter	*The kitchen maid*
Clothes	Bright, colourful cloth using expensive materials (linen, wool, silk) and dyes (red, blue, purple); made for her with embroidery and trimmings; fashionable; several sets.	Dull colours (greys and browns); itchy, rough material; made herself or handed down; one set of clothes.
Sleeping/living arrangements	Chamber, such as the solar; wooden furniture, for example the bed; linen sheets, furs, a mattress, hangings; decorated walls, tapestries; a fireplace; a window with window seat and maybe glass.	Slept on the floor or on a straw pallet, if lucky, in the kitchen or scullery as near to the fire as possible; dark, not many windows, no good light; some covering if there was any to hand.
Food	Rich variety; choicest cuts; plenty of meat; sweet things; wine; spiced and decorated.	Whatever she could get and whatever was left over – not much in winter.
Education	Educated by mother or other women; learned how to sew/ weave/spin/embroider; learned how to run household, keep accounts, in charge of the still room; perhaps able to read.	Not a lot, if any; may have had some idea of Bible stories from the windows in church.
Pastimes	Sewing, music, dancing, reading romances.	She would not have had time as she was always working.
Future	Marry into another rich family, marry young (14 years old); perhaps become a nun.	Servant all her life; might marry but her husband would also be poor.
Causes of death	Disease; childbirth.	Disease; childbirth; hunger/ malnutrition; overwork.

PHOTOCOPIABLE

PERIODS BEYOND LIVING MEMORY: **Castles in the Middle Ages**
What happened when the castle was attacked? Page 57

Name _____   Date _____

Why castles were attacked

Here are a number of reasons to explain why castles might have been attacked in the Middle Ages.
Can you recognise the right reasons? Write **f**, **p** or **t** next to the sentences.

f = false   **p** = possible   **t** = true

Armies attacked castles because…

1. …the king was bored and it was his playtime ☐

2. …they were bullies ☐

3. …they wanted to control the area ☐

4. …the castles were there and they were big ☐

5. …the people in the castles were the enemy ☐

6. …they wanted to increase their own wealth and power ☐

7. …they were invading the country ☐

8. …they didn't like the way it was decorated ☐

9. …their lord told them to do it ☐

10. …they thought it might be a good laugh ☐

Weapons for attacking the castle

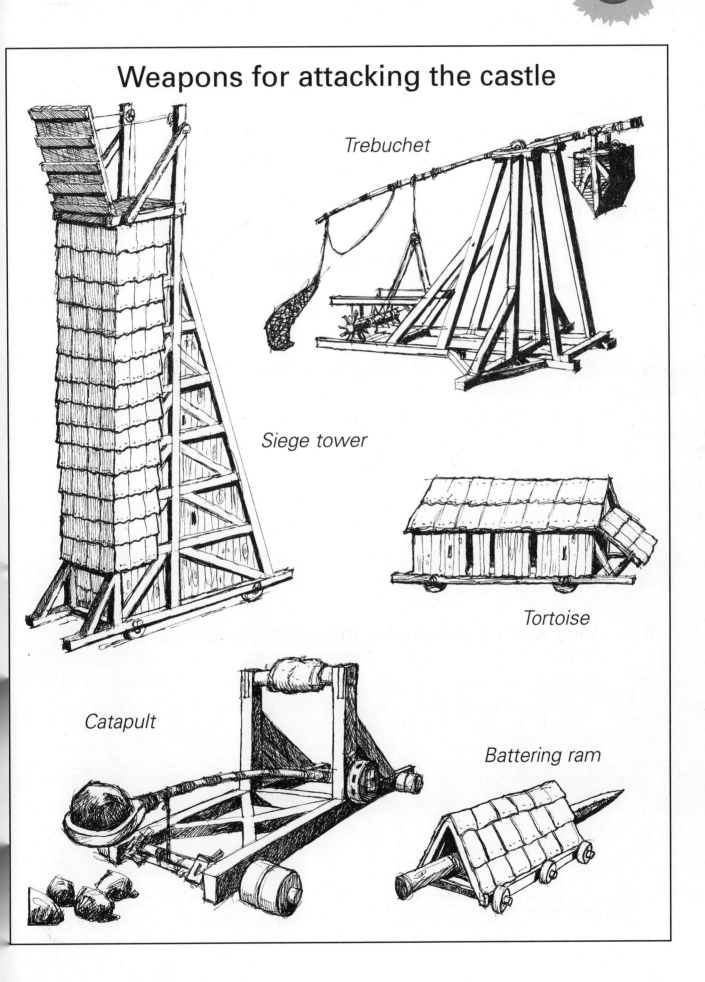

Trebuchet

Siege tower

Tortoise

Catapult

Battering ram

Bearcub and the blackberries

Bearcub was a boy – his real name was Brownbear. He was called Brownbear because a bear had been seen near the camp the day he was born, but they called him Bearcub because he was only six. He was picking blackberries. He had a basket that his mother had made from small branches and he was supposed to be collecting the berries to take back to camp. Actually he was eating them as fast as he picked them. All the women and children were out together, and he could hear them around him in the woods, talking and laughing as they picked, but the trees and bushes were very thick so he could not see anyone and they could not see him. They had been out all afternoon, and soon he got bored with picking and eating so he sat down in a space between the bushes. He was hot and tired and he decided to curl up and have a little sleep.

When he woke up it was getting dark and he could not hear any human voices around. He could hear wood pigeons cooing in the trees above, and the scuffling of a shrew as it scuttled away, and the snuffling of a hedgehog stirring under the bush. A slow-worm was slithering down near the stream, looking for slugs for its supper. Bearcub lay still and listened. He loved the woods and he was not scared to be alone. The grandmother had taught him that the animals and trees were all his brothers and sisters and he knew everything he needed was all around him. When he was thirsty he went to the stream and lapped up the cool water. When he was hungry

there were always things to eat. Now, at the end of summer, there were berries and crab apples. In winter the women dug for roots and went to their stores of nuts. Sometimes the family went on a walk for three days to the seaside and had a party with shellfish for dinner. Every week or so the men went hunting and if they were lucky everyone stuffed themselves on roast meat till they could eat no more.

Sometimes there was nothing but beetles or woodlice to eat, but Bearcub thought they were nice too.

Bearcub listened to the noises of the wood for a while, then he began to feel cold. He was only wearing a deerskin tied around his waist and he thought it would be best to go back to camp and sit by the fire. In the evening there was always a nice big fire and the whole family of mothers and fathers and children would all sit around to tell stories. Sometimes the grandmother would tell about how the world began, or the grandfather told funny stories about how Fox played tricks on all the other animals. Sometimes one of the men told a story of how he had been attacked by wolves when he was hunting and boasted about how brave he was. Usually one of the women would begin a song, and everyone would clap the rhythm and join in the chorus while she made up words about the things that had happened that day.

Bearcub got up and started off towards the camp. He was not lost even though it was quite dark now. He always knew where the camp was. He was used to looking for signs and listening for sounds and smelling for scents. He could smell the fire from a long way off. Then he decided to have an adventure.

He knew the family would not be very worried yet – no one had seen any bears or wolves around recently and they knew that Bearcub would not be far away. But he knew he would get into trouble for not collecting any blackberries – what is more he had left his basket behind. If he had an adventure then everyone would be so interested that they would forget about the blackberries and the basket. There was no time to have a real adventure, so Bearcub made an adventure in his head.

PERIODS BEYOND LIVING MEMORY: Life in the Stone Age

PHOTOCOPIABLE   What happened in Bearcub's adventure? Page 63

Bearcub's adventure

Bearcub sat down and closed his eyes to make an adventure happen in his head. He liked to have his adventures in a special place called the dream country and first he had to get there. He concentrated hard till he could see a little path between the trees; he imagined his bare feet feeling the grass on the path. He could hear the rustling of leaves and the wind in the trees. In his dream he imagined that the rustling turned into whispers because in the dream country the trees could talk and they muttered to one another forever about the doings of the animals, the coming and going of the birds and the taste of the rain that year. Bearcub hurried on into his dream adventure down the twisty path to find what he would find. Then he heard a new sound, "Click, click, crack," up ahead. "Click, click, click, crack," it got louder. Then suddenly he came out of the trees into a grassy clearing, an open space with trees all around. In the middle of the clearing crouched an old man. He was dressed in a big grey wolfskin cloak and his grey hair and beard matched so he looked like a cross between a man and a wolf. He was looking down at his lap as he worked away at something. "Click, crack," came the noise again.

"What are you doing, old Wolfman?" said Bearcub.

"Making dream arrows to shoot dream deer," said old Wolfman, who did not seem surprised to see Bearcub.

Wolfman had a round stone in one hand and a longer flatter stone in the other. He cracked the round stone down hard on the other and broke off a thin sharp piece. "Stand back out of the way, Bearcub, or a piece of flint will hit you in the eye," said Wolfman.

"I know that," said Bearcub. "I have seen the men make arrows lots of times."

Wolfman took the thin sharp piece of flint in his hand and began to press it against the other stone to break off bits until it was shaped like a leaf. Then he took a straight stick he had ready and dipped it

PERIODS BEYOND LIVING MEMORY: **Life in the Stone Age**

What happened in Bearcub's adventure? Page 63   **PHOTOCOPIABLE**

into some sticky sap from a tree and attached the arrowhead to the stick. He took a feather and cut it in half along the quill, and stuck the halves each side of the arrow.

Wolfman stood up and picked up his dream bow and his new dream arrows. "Let's go hunting, Bearcub," he said and immediately ran off through the trees, making no noise at all. Bearcub was taken by surprise for a second then he ran after him as quickly as he could. Wolfman dodged and dived and slipped between the oaks and the ashes and the birch and the hazel. Bearcub could only just keep the grey shape in sight. Then it disappeared completely.

Bearcub ran on blindly for a minute then he stopped bewildered in the darkest thickest part of the dream wood and listened. "Quickly to your left," whispered a slim silver birch tree. "Quietly now," rustled the tall, straight ash tree. "Be brave and strong," growled the great oak. Bearcub hurried on.

Suddenly he saw it. There was a stream, and drinking at the stream was a beautiful silvery white deer. At the same moment, he saw Wolfman hiding behind a bush with his bow and arrow ready. Bearcub knew that he must be very quiet on a hunt, and he knew that they had to hunt deer to get meat and skin for clothes. But in the dream he realised that this was not an ordinary deer. It was the Deermother. If she were killed then there would be no more deer for his people to hunt.

Bearcub jumped up. "Run away Deermother!" he shouted. Deermother turned and looked at him then flashed away through the trees. Wolfman howled with anger and charged towards Bearcub. Bearcub turned and ran. He ran and ran in and out of the muttering trees with the panting Wolfman behind getting closer and closer. Bearcub could see the light of his family's camp-fire now through the trees. Then he felt a hand on his shoulder.

"Wake up, Bearcub," said his mother. "Come and lie down by the fire, it is time to sleep."

"I have had an adventure," said Bearcub.

"Tell us in the morning," said his mother.

PHOTOCOPIABLE

PERIODS BEYOND LIVING MEMORY: Life in the Stone Age
What happened in Bearcub's adventure? Page 63

Bearcub's adventure

Bearcub hurried on down the twisty path.

In the middle of the clearing crouched an old man.

"I am making dream arrows to shoot dream deer," said old Wolfman.

"Let's go hunting, Bearcub."

He saw a beautiful silvery white deer and Wolfman hiding behind a bush, with his bow and arrow ready.

"Run away, Deermother!" he shouted.

Bearcub paints a picture

In the morning, Bearcub was woken by spots of rain on his face. He sniffed and smelled the lovely warm, smoky smell of the camp-fire. He wriggled down under the big bearskin his mother had put over him last night. He opened his eyes and looked around. Mother was crouched by his side, carefully placing more dry sticks to wake up the fire. His sister was bringing water from the stream in a basket lined with clay. His father and uncles were sitting on the ground, talking seriously. "They are planning a hunt," thought Bearcub. He knew that hunting needed a lot of talking first, and that the men often sat around for days before they actually went off with their bows and arrows. Today, though, they looked really serious. Since his dream adventure Bearcub felt like a man, so he got up and went over to them.

"What do you want, Bearcub?" said Uncle Badger.

"I had an adventure last night and now I am a man, so I am coming hunting," said Bearcub. All the men laughed.

"Run along Bearcub, you are too small, the wolves would eat you up in one gulp."

"But let me tell you about my adventure," said Bearcub.

"Shoo," said his father. So Bearcub had to shoo.

"Mother, last night I saved the Deermother from Wolfman," said Bearcub.

"Really dear?" said his mother. "Fetch some more dry sticks."

So Bearcub had to go into the woods and look for sticks. He knew that it was no good picking up wood from the ground, because it would be wet and would not burn, so he looked for dead branches low down on the trees. As he looked, he thought how he could make everyone listen to his story. Then he had an idea.

Bearcub decided to paint his adventure. He would paint Deermother first. He took some charcoal from the fire and mixed it with water to paint the black lines. He took some chalk from the path and ground it with a stone. Then he mixed that with some water to make the white fur. He found some brown clay for her eyes. Mashed up leaves made a green colour for the forest. He found a feather for a brush, but he knew he could use his fingers as well. The family tent was made of deerskin with the fur rubbed off. The outside was a creamy white colour. Since the rain had stopped and everyone was off doing something Bearcub started to paint his adventure on the side of the tent.

You can look for other natural things that make paints. You could paint on grey paper pinned up on the wall.

Bearcub's axe

It was time to move, summer was over and Bearcub's family were heading for the seaside and their autumn camp. The skin tents were folded into bundles tied on the women's backs, other useful things were put in baskets carried by the children. The men carried only their bows and arrows or hunting spears. The fire was put out by scraping earth over it.

Bearcub's basket was full. He had the deerskin which he wrapped around himself to sleep, his wooden digging stick for finding roots to eat, his bone whistle and his painting kit. On top he put his hand axe. His father had made this from nice dark-grey flint. It was small enough to fit in his hand and was chipped to a point. You could not cut down a tree with it but you could peck a notch in the side of a branch until it would break off. The basket was heavy and Bearcub had to crouch down to get it onto his back. As he stood up, his precious axe fell out of the basket onto the ground. Bearcub did not notice as he hurried after his family.

The camp lay empty and the wind blew leaves from the trees around to cover the ground and hide the lost axe. The rains came and turned the leaves to a soggy mass over it. The soggy leaves crumbled and turned into earth. A year later when Bearcub's people returned the axe was buried and no one noticed it.

There it lay under the earth for a thousand years, then another thousand as the world changed above it. The forest was cut down and fields and farms grew up all around. Six thousand years later a city had been built and houses and shops and schools stood where Bearcub had camped in the great forest. Still his stone axe was hidden under the ground.

The children at Oakland School were losing half their playground. A new nursery was being built and, behind the fence, a big yellow JCB was digging a trench. The driver had a bright orange hard hat and he was brilliant at controlling the huge digger. Suddenly he stopped the engine and jumped out. He stepped down into the hole and scrabbled about a bit. "Look kids," he called as he stepped out. "I thought I saw something." He held out a pointed stone about ten centimetres long. "Do you know what this is?" he said.

Do you?

Name _____   Date _____

Shops in the past

What is the address of the shop?

_____

_____

_____

What is the name of the shopkeeper? _____

What type of shop have you found? _____

What sort of goods are sold? _____

_____

Do you think people will come into the shop once a day, once a week or only on rare occasions? Why?

Write down or draw three things that you might find in the shop.

Would you like to shop there? Why do you think this? Write on the back of this sheet.

PERIODS WITHIN LIVING MEMORY: Shopping when Granny was a little girl

PHOTOCOPIABLE   How could I pay for my purchases? Page 76

Shopping then and now

A visit to the drapers in the 1930s

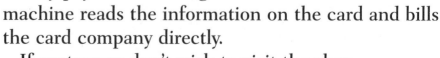

The customer passed between the front windows of
the main shop before entering along a sort of
passageway with various departments:
haberdashery, clothes, dress materials, silks, satins
and children's shoes. Each department had a shopwalker who walked
between the counters and was on hand to deal with any difficulties. When
the shop assistant had completed a sale, details were made in his book and
he would then call out, "Sign please." The shopwalker would check the bill
and sign it. The bill was torn out of the book, folded and placed into a
hollow wooden spherical ball which was then placed in a little cage. This
was lifted and fed out onto an overhead runway that guided it to the cash
desk in the middle of the shop. Here the account was entered into a sales
ledger then signed, receipted and any change enclosed. The little spherical
carrier was dispatched back to its starting point. Here the contents were
taken out by the sales assistant and handed over to the customer.

A visit to the supermarket in 2000

The customer enters the shop through the automatic doors. The shop is
huge, light and airy with open-plan aisles and counters piled high with
fruit and vegetables, both home-grown and exotic. The customer selects
their goods, scanning in the amount they cost with a bar-code reader. They
put their purchases straight into the trolley or basket. At the end of the
shopping trip they feed in the information from the scanner and receive an
automated itemised bill. They pay for this using their credit card – the

machine reads the information on the card and bills
the card company directly.

   If customers don't wish to visit the shop
themselves they can select, order and pay for their
chosen items through the Internet from their home
or office.

PERIODS WITHIN LIVING MEMORY: **Coming and going**

Why did people come to this country from the Caribbean? Page 80

PHOTOCOPIABLE

Name _____   Date _____

Why people came

People came to this country from the Caribbean for many different reasons. Here are some of the real reasons that people gave about why they came.

Sam King, Arthur Curling and Clinton Edwards fought for Britain in the war and came back to help rebuild the country.

Lucile Harris came to join her husband who was already working in this country.

John Richards wanted to travel. He knew about Britain from school and wanted to see what it was like.

Vince Reid was only 13 when he came with his family. His father thought they had the chance of a better life in Britain.

Oswald Denniston found that the special fare was cheap and he hoped that there would be plenty of jobs to choose from when he got here.

Give two reasons why people came to this country.

●

●

If you had been living in the Caribbean at this time, explain why you might have left.

How do you think you would have felt about leaving your home and why do you think you might have felt like this? Write on the back of this sheet.

PERIODS WITHIN LIVING MEMORY: **Coming and going**

PHOTOCOPIABLE   What did people do when they came? Page 83

Name _____   Date _____

On the buses now and when Granny was little

Look at the two pictures below and then answer the questions.

What two things do you think were the same about the two buses and how they were run?

●

●

What two things do you think were different about the two buses and how they were run?

●

●

Which bus would you like to travel on and why do you think this?

PERIODS WITHIN LIVING MEMORY: **Coming and going**

What was life like for those who came? Page 85

PHOTOCOPIABLE

Sandra's story

My Father left for England first. I remember the preparations for his going but not his actual departure. He was going to live with his sister who was already over there. He worked in the construction business first, rebuilding sites shattered by bomb damage. It was a dangerous business, however, as safety regulations were not really enforced. Many of his friends were injured and some even killed, so just before my mother went out to join him he became a guard with British Rail. I remember my mother's going because my little brother cried for days afterwards.

We moved to live with my grandmother in her big wooden brightly painted house. There was a wide veranda to sit on in the evenings and a deep space under the house that we all used to play in. My mother's family owned land and all my uncles and aunts lived in a little colony around my grandmother's house. There was always someone to play with and talk to. My Caribbean childhood passed in a blur of sunlight and colour. Every morning, my grandmother would tightly plait my sister's and my hair, ensure that we were tidy in our blue and white uniforms and then give us a large spoonful of cod-liver oil before we went to school! The only good thing about it was the piece of orange, freshly picked from the garden, that we were allowed afterwards. But nothing really took the taste away.

In my last year at primary school I took my common entrance exam to see whether I could attend St Mary's High School. I was very excited when I passed because they had a really nice uniform with a straw hat which had a bright blue ribbon around it.

Lots of the lessons were given by nuns and they really intrigued me because I didn't know much about them. We used to see them flying past our road in their little Beetle car.

I never got to St Mary's, however, because in August we went to rejoin our parents in London. I don't recall much in detail about the immediate days and weeks prior to leaving Jamaica but I do remember the actual day we left. It was very hot and wet because it was the height of the hurricane season. I remember wondering if the plane would be able to take off. I felt sad leaving my grandmother because I knew she would be all on her own without any more grandchildren to look after.

The flight was very long and bewildering. My sister and I had new dresses that my mother had sent for us from London. We were all sick from drinking the pasteurised

orange juice. I suppose our systems were still used to those fresh oranges we used to pick from trees in our garden each day.

On arrival, London appeared to be one huge industrial estate, a sea of brown brick buildings with chimneys on top. Everything was so close together. I couldn't see how people could live so close to each other. We also had to get used to having a lot less space to roam around in and we had to be inside a lot more. There was no more fresh fruit from the garden. Having to be inside so much was a big shock to the system. Having to stay inside in the Caribbean meant you were either ill or it was bedtime or there was a hurricane raging.

We had to get used to being with Mum and Dad again and they had to get used to us. My mother spoiled my younger brother, who had been so little and cried so much when she had left. We had a new sister to get to know. My parents had had another daughter while we had been living with my grandmother. She was now toddling around.

We were in school for the start of the autumn term. Having to get to and from school by ourselves on the bus was scary. We had to memorise the landmarks very quickly. I remember thinking what an enormous building the school was. I thought that I would never find my way around it let alone get to lessons on time. I missed the routine of my Jamaican school. There was no whole-school assembly each morning, no hymns, no bible readings, no bells to announce the start or end of the day. There seemed no sense of being a school community. The school tuck shop had Wagon Wheels and crisps unlike the coconut cake, 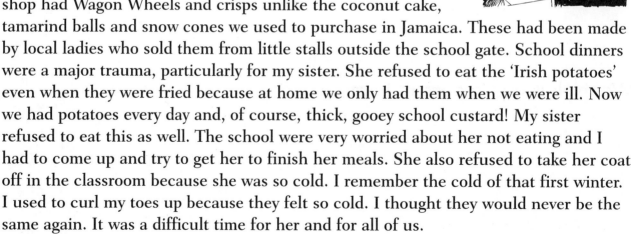 tamarind balls and snow cones we used to purchase in Jamaica. These had been made by local ladies who sold them from little stalls outside the school gate. School dinners were a major trauma, particularly for my sister. She refused to eat the 'Irish potatoes' even when they were fried because at home we only had them when we were ill. Now we had potatoes every day and, of course, thick, gooey school custard! My sister refused to eat this as well. The school were very worried about her not eating and I had to come up and try to get her to finish her meals. She also refused to take her coat off in the classroom because she was so cold. I remember the cold of that first winter. I used to curl my toes up because they felt so cold. I thought they would never be the same again. It was a difficult time for her and for all of us.

Sandra is now married with two children of her own. She and her husband live in South West London where they own and manage several nursery schools. All her brothers and sisters still live in London, as do her parents. Her father worked for British Rail for the rest of his working life.

Name _____   Date _____

The history of space exploration

We found out about:

It happened on:

The names of those involved were:

The country involved was:

We think it was important because:

We would like to find out more about:

PHOTOCOPIABLE

FAMOUS EVENTS
What was the race for space? Page 90

The history of space exploration

The first orbit of the Earth or Moon

The first space walk

The first man in space

The first creature in space

The first Moon landing

The first woman in space

Name _____   Date _____

Apollo 11 – preparing for the unknown

Tick the statements if you think they are correct:

The *Apollo 11* mission will land a man on the Moon. ☐

The mission will have a four-man crew. ☐

The *Apollo 11* mission will orbit the Sun. ☐

Apollo 11 will carry two flags to leave on the surface
of the Moon. ☐

The lunar module will land three men on the Moon. ☐

Apollo 11 will take off in the year 2001. ☐

Two astronaut explorers will land on the Moon. ☐

The astronauts will remain on the surface of the Moon
for a year. ☐

The astronauts will collect samples of the lunar surface. ☐

The mission badge is a rocket blasting off. ☐

The plaque left behind will read: "We come in peace
for all mankind." ☐

The two astronauts will look for Moon monsters. ☐

The great space debate

Points to support the resolution:

● Too many people have already given their lives through accidents in the past. No technological advance is worth people dying for it.

● Too much money has been spent already on this. We should spend the money trying to solve the problems on Earth.

● Countries explored space because they wanted to show that they were better than other countries. This is not a good reason for such a major undertaking.

● It is pointless – no good came from being able to land a man on the Moon.

● Astronauts may bring back horrible diseases from Mars and everyone on Earth will catch them and die.

● We might discover alien life forms who want to fight with us.

● We have made a mess of Earth, we should not do the same with Space. We have already left a lot of litter, such as lunar modules and buggies, on the Moon.

● There are still areas of the Earth, such as the oceans, that we haven't fully explored yet.

The great space debate

Points to oppose the resolution:

● If we don't carry on then we limit the achievements of all the brave people in the past, such as Neil Armstrong, who were willing to take risks on our behalf.

● We could use resources from the Moon or Mars and conserve those of Earth.

● Telecommunications, effective weather forecasting and the World Wide Web are only possible because of the satellites we have put into space.

● Experiments performed in space and the technology designed for use in space have already made our lives better.

● If the population of the Earth and the pressure on its resources continues to grow we may need to move into space.

● We might discover alien life forms who want to help us and be our friends.

● Some things are easier and more cost effective to build in space.

● Mankind has always been an explorer and this is 'the final frontier' as well as a great and glorious adventure.

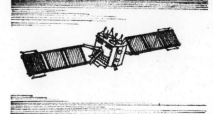

PHOTOCOPIABLE

FAMOUS EVENTS
What happened on Uncle Pliny's resuce mission? Page 96

Cornelius Tacitus
Rome

Dear Cornelius

Thank you for your letter asking me to tell you about my uncle. I am glad that you are going to write about him in your history book. It is true he died when the volcano erupted at Pompeii.

My uncle was in charge of the navy ships at Misenum. It was the early afternoon of the 24th August. He had been out in the hot sun, so he took a cold bath, then after lunch he went to work, writing his book. My mother called him outside to show him a big cloud that appeared in the sky. It was shaped like a huge tree coming out of the mountain.

Uncle decided to go and get a better look, so he told one of his sailors to bring a boat. He asked me to go with him but I was reading a book and I did not want too. I was only eighteen then. As he came out of the house, a slave ran up with a letter. It was from his friend's wife. She said that the volcano was erupting and she asked Uncle to bring his ships to rescue the people.

Uncle ordered his men to put up the sails immediately. He was very brave. Everyone else was running away but he led his ships right into the most dangerous place. Hot ashes were falling from the sky, then stones came crashing down. The sailors wanted to go back but he made them go on. They got to shore and started to rescue some people but then the wind blew so hard and the sea got so rough that they could not get to sea again. The sky was black now and stones and ash were pouring down, blocking the roads and smashing the roofs of the houses. They could see flashes of fire on the mountain.

Uncle tried to keep everyone calm by pretending that everything would be all right. He even lay down and had some dinner. They went back to the beach but the ships were still not able to sail away. Suddenly my uncle collapsed, choking from the smoke.

That is how my uncle died. I hope you will write about him so that people will remember him in the future.

Best wishes
Your friend
Gaius Plinius

Name _____   Date _____

Research focus sheet

Use your information source to help you find out about the disaster.

Tick the type of source that you have.

☐ *burial record*   ☐ *eyewitness account*   ☐ *official report*

☐ *newspaper report*   ☐ *photograph*   ☐ *picture*

What is the name of your character?

What does he or she do?

Give a brief account of what you have found out:

What is your evidence for this?

How do you feel about what happened?

Why do you feel this?

Shaneenee's story

I was travelling back from Lebanon to my home in America. Three of my cousins were with me – they were going to America to get jobs in a factory. My young niece Banoura was with us too. The *Titanic* was a wonderful ship, it was so big. We were in the cheap cabins down below but even there it was nice and comfortable. The Lebanese people shared a dining room so we had a nice time eating together and having fun. The rich people were in a different part of the ship but sometimes we saw them in their beautiful clothes and we heard the bands playing for their dances. We had our own music of course.

On Sunday night I had gone to bed. There was a tremendous crash that shook the ship. I jumped out of bed in my nightclothes and ran into the corridor. People were crowding into the passageways trying to get up on deck. I went to look in my cousins' room but they were gone. Then I saw Banoura. I grabbed her and pulled her with me. Some sailors came down and made us put on life preservers. Then some of the rich men passengers in beautiful suits helped push us up onto the deck.

Everybody was confused and scared. My cousin George was on deck and he pushed us towards one of the lifeboats. They were only letting women and children get into it because there was not enough room for everyone. Some men were trying to get into the boats but sailors with guns stopped them. Everyone was terrified. Some people jumped into the freezing cold water, other people were too scared to move.

The boat was full of women in their nightclothes. It was very cold. One lady was crying because she had lost her little boy, Tommy. One frightened young man had managed to get into the boat and we hid him from the sailors so that they would not throw him out. The sailors started to row away from the *Titanic*. We had not got very far away when we saw the lights of the big ship go out then it slipped down under the water.

We were six hours in that boat. It was so cold. Some women set fire to their straw hats and held them up, hoping that another ship would see the light and rescue us. Early next morning we saw a ship coming to save us. I was too cold to climb up the ladder into it and they had to pull me up. They pulled the children up in baskets.

The best thing was, a few hours later I saw a nurse carrying a little boy. It was Tommy! So I was able to take him back to his mother.

Banoura and I eventually got to America safely but I will never forget the *Titanic*.